DANIEL 11

DANIEL 11:

A Message for God's End-time People

Perry F. Louden, Jr

XULON PRESS

Xulon Press
2301 Lucien Way #415
Maitland, FL 32751
407.339.4217
www.xulonpress.com

Xulon PRESS

Paperback ISBN-13: 978-1-66284-445-4
Ebook ISBN-13: 978-1-66284-446-1

Table of Contents

Special thanks for encouragement and special services:

Becki Louden, my encouraging wife
Pastor Dennis Clark, Scriptural advising
Richard Lamb, Scriptural advising
Jesse Ravencroft, Scriptural advising
Suzan Warren, editing
Betsy Phillips, editing
And above all, *Jesus,* my Lord and Savior

Clovis I being baptized by St. Remy

"For such a time as this."
Mordecai to Queen Esther, c.a. 475 BC

Introduction:
Searching *"to and fro"*
in the Book of Daniel

But you, Daniel, shut up the words and seal the book,
until the time of the end. Many shall run to and fro,
and knowledge shall increase. —Daniel 12:4

IN MY EARLY twenties, I was in the Army Reserve and had to get a haircut before a weekend drill. Being on my own and not having much money, I would get my hair cuts at a barber school and then just pay the student hairstylist a tip. I noticed the stylist-in-training cut one side, then the back, then the other side, and finally the top. He finished, and I thought it looked great, but the instructor came over to check it. She did not go around the sides then the top. She started on one side of my forehead and worked back to the opposite side, then she started on the opposite side and went back, making an X across the top of my head in a crisscross shape. I could not believe how much hair was missed by the student stylist!

In the same way, we generally study the book of Daniel chapter by chapter. While we can learn much from that technique, we can also "run to and fro" in the book and increase our knowledge and understanding by studying the book of Daniel chronologically, empire by empire across the four major prophecies. When studying and teaching Daniel chapter by chapter, we continue to back up and review what came in a previous chapter to understand the chapter we are focusing on. Yet, when looking at the prophecies chronologically, we can gain incredible insights and understandings with a fuller presentation of each kingdom and its time. My original goal was simply to learn more about Daniel and possibly create a new Bible study series on Daniel. My study resulted in a unique position for interpreting verses. 23 to 39—The Rome and Constantinople position.

What follows is a position of Daniel 11 that came out of a study on Daniel chronologically, empire by empire, and not tge usual chapter by chapter study. This method of studying kingdom by kingdom worked well for the first four empires, and one can easily see the start and end of Babylon, Medo-Persia, Greece, and Rome in Daniel 2, 7, 8, 9, and even in chapter 11. However, the divided kingdoms were missing, or obscured, in Daniel 11. After checking commentaries, biblical scholars, and online research, I discovered no agreement on this portion of Scripture. Through much prayer and diligent study, a parallel to Daniel 2 was found in Daniel 11. This study in the following pages will explore those parallels.

Daniel 2 pictures the toes as the final kingdom just before the Rock of God strikes the image and grinds it to powder. We are at the toenails of the image, looking back over the entirety of human history from 605 BC to the present. The next and final kingdom will be Jesus' eternal kingdom. All the prophecies in the book of Daniel have the power and vitality of the living God of heaven. Daniel gives a message of hope in the judgment—God always wins!

Before moving on to the study, I would like to briefly address two vital principles: first, the separation of the Christian church and state, and second, individual freedom of conscience. The former we have today because the Founders of our great nation placed this principle at the very onset of the U.S. Constitution. The latter, freedom of conscience, was handed down to us by the Protestant Reformers. They gave their blood, and at times, their lives to wrest freedom of conscience from the church-state power of their time. Both principles are under assault today. Our Christian Founders established a religious nation based on Judeo-Christian princi-ples where all people could follow the dictates of their conscience. However, many today want to see our country become the twen-ty-first century Christendom. We must raise our voices against this movement, pointing to the horrific record of the past. At the same time, we must encourage others to search the Scriptures for themselves with love and long-suffering, and act upon their individual consciences. Ms. Nancy, a wise lady from our church who is now resting in Jesus, once said, "Others may, but I may not," and that is the essence of freedom of conscience.

Rules for Interpretation

Consistent principles of interpretation are the hallmark of suc-cessfully understanding of the message God that has for us in prophecy. The positions set forth are predicated on time-tested methods of biblical interpretation.

For this study, rules for the interpretation of the book of Daniel include: (1) Using Daniel chapter 2 as the template for understanding the other three prophecies in the book of Daniel; (2) understanding that prophecies are often repeated and enlarged upon; and (3) allowing the Bible to interpret itself by using the immediate context first, then moving out to surrounding passages, the rest of Daniel, and finally, to the whole Bible, especially any words of Jesus that may apply.

Parallel Prophecies

Daniel crafts his prophecies in parallels, which are seen throughout his book. Chapters 2 and 7, written predominately in Aramaic, parallel each other and discuss secular world empires. The prophecies in chapters 8–9 and 10–12 again parallel each other and discuss the sanctuary ministry and the covenant. Unlike the prophecies in chapters 2 and 7, these final two prophecies were written predominately in Hebrew.

Observations on the four prophecies of Daniel

Several observations are apparent in the four principal prophecies. First, the prophecies in Daniel 2 and 7 focus on the beginning and end of each empire. Still, there is some mixing of iron and clay in Daniel 2, and the horns grew out of the beast's head in Daniel 7 coming out of the Roman period into the Divided

Kingdoms. This includes characteristics and generalities regarding the empire. Next, the prophecy in Daniel 8–9 focuses on God's people, the temple, and the Sanctuary service, which is crucial to understanding Daniel 10–12. Finally, the prophecy of Daniel 10–12 focuses on the overall shifts in the balance of power (not necessarily the end of the kingdom) and on how kings and kingdoms affect God's people and the ministry of the temple.

Daniel 2 Political Divisions

We often see Nebuchadnezzar's image as having five political divisions—(1) head, (2) chest and arms, (3) belly and thighs, (4) legs, and (5) feet. Yet, there are actually six divisions in Daniel 2. Notice the distinction between feet and the toes found in vv. 41–42,

> *And as you saw the **feet and toes**, partly of potter's clay and partly of iron, it shall be a divided kingdom, but some of the firmness of iron shall be in it, just as you saw iron mixed with the soft clay. And as the **toes of the feet** were partly iron and partly clay, so the kingdom shall be partly strong and partly brittle.*

Toes have toenails at the end, and if Jesus's return is at the door, we must be at the tip of the toenails of Nebuchadnezzar's image.

Our six political divisions from Daniel 2 are as follows:

Head	Babylon	605 BC—538 BC
Chest and Arms	Medo-Persia	538 BC—331 BC

Belly and Thighs	Greece	331 BC—31 BC
Legs	Rome	31 BC— AD 476
Feet	Medieval Divided Kingdoms	AD 476—1798
Toes	End-Time Divided Kingdoms	1798—End

These six political divisions and time periods will guide us throughout the remaining three prophecies in Daniel. We will primarily be referencing Daniel 2 with its parallels in Daniel 11, yet, in the following chart, we can see a basic breakdown of all six empires in each of Daniels four major prophecies:

Prophecy Divisions by Empire

Empire	Daniel 2	Daniel 7	Daniel 8–9	Daniel 10–12
Babylon	32, 37–38	4, 12, 17	n/a	n/a
Medo-Persia	32, 39	5, 12, 17	8:3, 4, 14, 20, 26; 9:23–25	2
Greece	32, 39	6, 12, 17	8:6–8, 21–22	3–19
Imperial Rome	33, 40	7, 12, 17, 19, 23	8:9, 10a, 23* 9:26, 27a	20–22
Medieval Divided Kingdoms	33b, 41–43	8, 20–21, 24–25	8:10–14, 23*–26; 9:27c	23–39
End-Time Divided Kingdoms	43, 42, 44	9–11, 22, 26, 27	25	40–45

*Imperial and Medieval Kingdoms are mingled in these verses.

Stages of Prophetic History

1. Babylonian Empire (605 - 539BC)

Daniel 2	Daniel 7	Daniel 8-9	Daniel 10-12
		N/A	N/A

2. Medo-Persian Empire (539 - 331BC)

Daniel 2	Daniel 7	Daniel 8-9	Daniel 10-12
			Cyrus Delivers God's People

3. Greek Empire (331 - 31BC)

Daniel 2	Daniel 7	Daniel 8-9	Daniel 10-12
			KON - Seleucid Dynasty KOS - Ptolemaic Dynasty

4. Roman Empire (31BC - 476 AD)

Daniel 2	Daniel 7	Daniel 8-9	Daniel 10-12
			Imperial Rome arises and destroys the Prince of the Covenant

5. Medieval Divided Kingdoms (476 - 1798)

Daniel 2	Daniel 7	Daniel 8-9	Daniel 10-12
			KON – Rome Church-State Union KOS – Constantinople Church-State Union

6. End-Time Divided Kingdoms (1798 - 2ⁿᵈ Coming)

Daniel 2	Daniel 7	Daniel 8-9	Daniel 10-12
			Spiritual Rome attempts to destroy the People of the Covenant

7. God's Eternal Kingdom

Daniel 2	Daniel 7	Daniel 8-9	Daniel 10-12
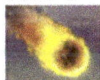			Michael Delivers God's People

Guidelines for the Interpretation of Daniel 11

Daniel 11 presents some unique challenges for interpretation that we must take into consideration for proper understanding. While some texts have incredible detail, others exhibit an extreme amount of obscurity. Take v. 23 for example: "*And from the time* (what time?) *that an alliance* (which alliance?) *is made by him* (who?) *he* (who?) *shall act deceitfully, and he* (which he?) *shall become strong with a small people* (Romans? Jews? someone else?)." For this verse and many like it, the old adage of context is king must be applied.

While some passages are obscure, we do know without a doubt that Jesus is at the center of Daniel 11. We read in v. 22, "*Armies shall be utterly swept away before him and broken, **even the prince of the covenant.**"* Just as Jesus is the Messiah (or anointed one) the Prince in Daniel 9:25, we see Jesus here as the true prince of the covenant. Before v. 22, the focus is on God's people in the literal Jewish nation, while the verses after v. 22 focus on God's spiritual Jews in the Christian church. (See Rom. 2:28–29)

Daniel 11 has several compass texts. These are texts that give us a sense of location and direction in the chapter. A verse from the prophecy may fit its historical situation nearly perfectly. We can see this in v. 5, "*Then the king of the south* (Ptolemy I Soter) *shall be strong, but one of his princes* (Seleucus Nicator) *shall be stronger than he and shall rule, and his authority shall be a great authority* (the Seleucid kingdom became much larger and more powerful than the Ptolemaic kingdom)."

Examples of Compass Texts:

- Verse 3 "do as he wills"

- Verse 16 "as he wills"

- Verse 22 "the prince of the covenant"

- Verse 36 "as he wills"

- Verse 40 "At the time of the end"

The compass texts with the phrase "do as he wills" designates a new king or kingdom has arisen. We read in v. 3, "*Then a mighty king* (Alexander the Great) *shall arise, who shall rule with great dominion and do as he wills.*"

The Real Power Behind Earthly Empires

We do not find references to Lucifer, Satan, or the devil mentioned in Daniel; even so, we know clearly from Isaiah 14 the power behind Babylon, and hence all worldly powers is indeed Lucifer, the "Son of the Morning" (Isa. 14:12). He represents all earthly kingdoms. Yet, we do see a short period during the time of King Cyrus where the God of heaven overruled Satan's influence on a nation. Cyrus typifies Michael's kingdom and deliverer of God's people in the prophecy of Daniel 10–12. Under King Cyrus, the Jews returned home and all the nations in the empire could worship their gods without interference from the ruling kingdom. In Daniel 10:13, we see the power of God behind the King of Persia, "*The prince of the kingdom of Persia withstood me twenty-one days, but Michael, one of the chief princes, came to help me, for I was left there with the kings of Persia.*" The exiles returned home under Persia's decrees for a time of peace with the protection and authority of the power of the day. Their conflicts often arose with the small nations around them who harassed them, but when they believed the promises of God and called on the Lord, they were able to overcome these trials through God's strength.

All the kingdoms of this world, including Babylon, Persia, Greece, Rome, the Medieval Divided Kingdoms, and the End-Time Divided Kingdoms, have Satan leading them. As such, God's people must be vigilant against the actions Satan will use in the name of the state. After all, it was Satan who conspired with the Jewish Sanhedrin and the Roman authorities in a church-state union to crucify Jesus, the prince of the covenant. It will likewise be Satan to inspire the world into false worship at the end of time. Yet, like Cyrus of old, Michael will arise and deliver God's people from the power of Satan.

1: The Prophecy of Daniel 10–12

And now I will show you the truth.
—Daniel 11:3

Introduction

WE READ IN Daniel 10:1, *"In the third year of Cyrus king of Persia a word was revealed to Daniel, who was named Belteshazzar. And the word was true, and it was a great conflict. And he understood the word and had understanding of the vision."*

The prophecy of chapters 10–12 begins with Daniel praying and mourning for his people, and the angel states the prophecy is a great battle or conflict. Daniel 11 is about great battles/conflicts centered on God's people. We need to ask two key questions: (1) what are these great battles/conflicts? and (2) where do we find God's people during these conflicts?

For the Latter Days

This vision in chapters 10–12 is for us in the latter days. The angel states in 10:14 that he came *"to make you (Daniel) understand what is to happen to your people in the **latter days**. For the vision*

1

is for days yet to come." Why did the angel talk so much on the Greek Kings of the North and South if the vision is about the end of time—our time? The answer must be that vv. 3–19 can help us interpret the parallel text of vv. 23–39 occurring after the cross. The writer of Hebrews states, *"Long ago, at many times and in many ways, God spoke to our fathers by the prophets, but in these **last days** he has spoken to us by his Son, whom he appointed the heir of all things, through whom also he created the world"* (Heb. 1:1–2). Thus, we have been in the last days since the cross, drawing ever closer and closer to Jesus's second coming.

Repeat and Enlarge

What about this statement, *"he* (Daniel) *understood the word and had understanding of the vision"*? Daniel explicitly states he understood the vision in chapter 11. However, in Daniel 8, we found that he did not understand that vision and needed more explanation which we find in chapter 9. Prior to that, in chapter 8 v. 27, we read, *"And I, Daniel, was overcome and lay sick for some days. Then I rose and went about the king's business, but **I was appalled by the vision and did not understand it.**"* In Daniel 9:22, we read, *"He made me understand, speaking with me and saying, "O Daniel, **I have now come out to give you insight and understanding.**"* Why would Daniel be able to understand this vision in Daniel 11 - that we have such a hard time understanding - but he could not understand about the 2,300 days. The answer lies in chapter 8, where Daniel understands what is called the "chazown" or general revelation vision, which was a repeat and enlargement of the scenes he had seen and Daniel 2 and 7. However, in what is called the "mar'eh" or the special "appearance" vision, he does not understand because it was not in Daniel 2 and 7. We also see Daniel asking for understanding about the *"time, times, and half a time"* in chapter 12, vv. 7 and 8. The only conclusion is that Daniel 11 must be a repetition and enlargement of what Daniel saw in the visions of chapters 2, 7, and 8–9. Nothing can be added in chapter 11, or Daniel would not have understood it. While they are undoubtedly true and may fit perfectly into Daniel's four prophecies, themes from Revelation cannot be interjected into Daniel 11. If they were, Daniel would certainly have asked the angel for an explanation. The point here is Daniel must have based his understanding on things he already knew or had seen in his earlier visions. The angel tells Daniel the "truth" of the great battles and conflicts of nations that will happen concerning Nebuchadnezzar's dream found in Daniel 2.

Checkmate!

Another unique aspect of Daniel 11 is when each kingdom ends. When the new kingdom stops the advance of the old kingdom, we have a shift at that point to the new kingdom, yet the old kingdom may live on for a time. In the game of chess, this is called a "checkmate," where a player's king is ready for capture, and there is no possible way of escape. Daniel 11:2 states, *"Behold, three more kings shall arise in Persia, and a fourth* (Xerxes I) *shall be far richer than all of them. And when he has become strong through his riches, he shall stir up all against the kingdom of Greece."* Xerxes lost to the Greeks at the Battles of Salamis and Plataea in ca 480 BC, and the power shifted to Rome even though seven more kings reigned in Medo-Persia. This differs from the previous prophecies in chapters 2 and 7, where the kingdoms end entirely, and the new kingdom begins. In Daniel 11, each kingdom ends when a new kingdom checkmates its power, and our attention then moves to the new kingdom.

Now let us compare empire collapses in Daniel 2 and 7 with the checkmate in Daniel 11. The former gives the total collapse of the empire, while the latter gives the rise of the next dominant power. We can visualize this in the following graph:

Empire	Beginning in Daniel 2 & 7	Checkmate in Daniel 11	End in Daniel 2 & 7
Babylon	605 BC	n/a	539 BC Cyrus conquers Babylon
Medo-Persia	539 BC	480 BC Battle of Thermopylae	331 BC Battle of Gaugamela
Greece	331 BC	188 BC Treaty of Apamea[1]	31 BC[2] Battle of Actium

---

[1] Not only did Antiochus III capitulate to Rome, but the Ptolemy Dynasty lost all its land holdings in Asia Minor to the Roman Republic. https://www.britannica.com/biography/Antiochus-III-the-Great#ref146980.

[2] Some could conclude the final remnants of the Greek Empire fell in 65 BC when Pompey put down the Greek Mithridates rebellion; others could conclude it fell in 31 BC at the Battle of Actium. However, the point should be made that Rome was the dominant power after 188 BC while the Greek Empire continued to decline and eventually was overcome completely.

Rome	31 BC	AD 31 Prince of the covenant crucified	AD 476 barbarian king Odoacer deposed the Roman emperor
Medieval Divided Kingdoms	AD 476	1798 Wounded by France	n/a*
End-Time Divided Kingdoms	1798	People of the Prince Delivered	2nd Coming

Based on Daniel 7 and 8, the power in the Medieval Kingdoms continues until the second coming of Christ.

In Daniel 8, we can clarify why there is a gap between the new power arising on the scene while the old power declines over time. We read in Daniel 8:12, *"As for the rest of the beasts, their dominion was taken away, but their lives were prolonged for a season and a time."* However, the previous verse is explicit: the final kingdom is the exception, going to the end of time and then ends immediately just before the second coming. Verse 11, *"I looked then because of the sound of the great words that the horn was speaking. And as I looked, the beast was killed, and its body destroyed and given over to be burned with fire."*

The Parallel Passages in Daniel 11

Daniel 11 has three sets of parallel passages, which we can see as follows:

(a) Medo-Persia/Everlasting Kingdom - Here, we have two deliverers in Cyrus and Michael. Isaiah 45:1 indicates that

Cyrus was a type of Christ, "*Thus says the Lord to his anointed, to Cyrus, whose right hand I have grasped, to subdue nations before him and to loose the belts of kings, to open doors before him that gates may not be closed.*"

(b) Greece Hellenism/Medieval Divided Kingdoms - Here, we have great kings who die in Alexander and Constantine and left a power vacuum between the Kings of the North and the Kings of the South.

(c) Imperial Rome/End-Time Divided Kingdoms - Here, we have a church-state death decree for the prince of the covenant and the people of the covenant.

Below is a comparison chart:

Medo-Persia v. 11:2—Cyrus was the deliverer from literal Babylon to usher in a time of peace with no KON or KOS

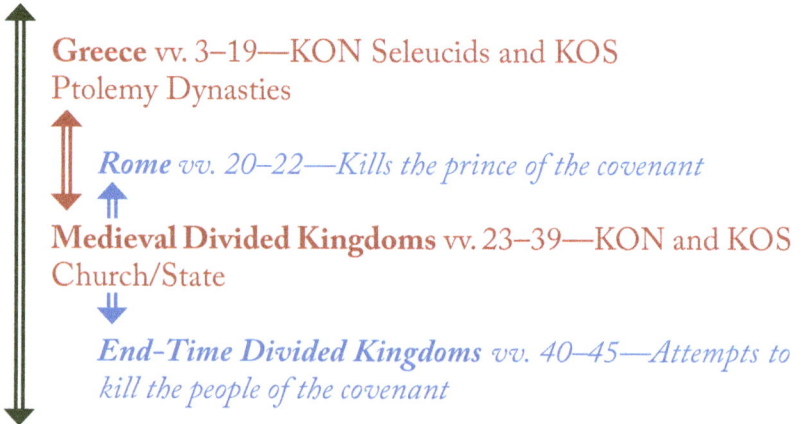

Greece vv. 3–19—KON Seleucids and KOS Ptolemy Dynasties

Rome vv. 20–22—Kills the prince of the covenant

Medieval Divided Kingdoms vv. 23–39—KON and KOS Church/State

End-Time Divided Kingdoms vv. 40–45—Attempts to kill the people of the covenant

Everlasting Kingdom v. 12:1—Michael will be the deliverer from spiritual Babylon and usher in a time of peace with no KON or KOS.

These parallel passages help to keep the interpretation on track by identifying similar keywords in the equivalent text. We apply these passages by detecting *similar* elements, such as the "king of the south" (vv. 5 and 25). Yet, we can see *opposite* elements with "mighty" (v. 3) and "deceitful" (v. 23). Additionally, the verse may be *superseded* by a prophetic element, as with Cyrus and Michael (vv. 11:2 and 12:1). That being said, texts referring to the parallel kingdom must not supplant the meaning of the primary kingdom's interpretation. The parallel text acts as our guardrail beside the road; we drive on the paved road between the lines and only need the guardrail to prevent us from going into the ditch.

While not intended to be a rigid, exegetical critique of the parallels in the Hebrew text, below, we see a loose layout of these parallel passages beside each other. Notice the similarities with its parallel text with similar words, contrasting, and comparative themes.

Cyrus the Great the Deliverer	Michael the Prince and Deliverer
11:2 And now I will show you the truth. Behold, three more kings shall arise in Persia, and a fourth shall be far richer than all of them. And when he has become strong through his riches, he shall stir up all against the kingdom of Greece.	12:1–3 At that time shall arise Michael, the great prince who has charge of your people. And there shall be a time of trouble, such as never has been since there was a nation till that time. But at that time your people shall be delivered, everyone whose name shall be found written in the book.
Mighty King, KON, and KOS	**Deceitful King, KON, and KOS**
11:3 Then a mighty king shall arise, who shall rule with great dominion and do as he wills.	11:23 And from the time that an alliance is made with him he shall act deceitfully, and he shall become strong with a small people.
4 And as soon as he has arisen, his kingdom shall be broken and divided toward the four winds of heaven, but not to his posterity, nor according to the authority with which he ruled, for his kingdom shall be plucked up and go to others besides these.	24 Without warning he shall come into the richest parts of the province, and he shall do what neither his fathers nor his fathers' fathers have done, scattering among them, spoil, and goods. He shall devise plans against strongholds, but only for a time.
5 Then the king of the south shall be strong, but one of his princes shall be stronger than he and shall rule, and his authority shall be a great authority.	25a And he shall stir up his power and his heart against the king of the south with a great army.
6a After some years they shall make an alliance, and the daughter of the king of the south shall come to the king of the north to make an agreement.	25b And the king of the south shall wage war with an exceedingly great and mighty army, but he shall not stand, for plots shall be devised against him.
6b But she shall not retain the strength of her arm, and he and his arm shall not endure, but she shall be given up, and her attendants, he who fathered her, and he who supported her in those times.	26 Even those who eat his food shall break him. His army shall be swept away, and many shall fall down slain.

7 And from a branch from her roots one shall arise in his place. He shall come against the army and enter the fortress of the king of the north, and he shall deal with them and shall prevail.	27 And as for the two kings, their hearts shall be bent on doing evil. They shall speak lies at the same table, but to no avail, for the end is yet to be at the time appointed.
8 He shall also carry off to Egypt their gods with their metal images and their precious vessels of silver and gold, and for some years he shall refrain from attacking the king of the north.	28 And he shall return to his land with great wealth, but his heart shall be set against the holy covenant. And he shall work his will and return to his own land.
9 Then the latter shall come into the realm of the king of the south but shall return to his own land.	29 At the time appointed he shall return and come into the south, but it shall not be this time as it was before.
10 His sons shall wage war and assemble a multitude of great forces, which shall keep coming and overflow and pass through, and again shall carry the war as far as his fortress.	30 For ships of Kittim shall come against him, and he shall be afraid and withdraw, and shall turn back and be enraged and take action against the holy covenant. He shall turn back and pay attention to those who forsake the holy covenant.
11 Then the king of the south, moved with rage, shall come out and fight against the king of the north. And he shall raise a great multitude, but it shall be given into his hand.	31 Forces from him shall appear and profane the temple and fortress, and shall take away the regular ~~burnt offering~~ (see note below). And they shall set up the abomination that makes desolate.
12 And when the multitude is taken away, his heart shall be exalted, and he shall cast down tens of thousands, but he shall not prevail.	32 He shall seduce with flattery those who violate the covenant, but the people who know their God shall stand firm and take action.
13 For the king of the north shall again raise a multitude, greater than the first. And after some years he shall come on with a great army and abundant supplies.	33 And the wise among the people shall make many understand, though for some days they shall stumble by sword and flame, by captivity and plunder.

14 In those times many shall rise against the king of the south, and the violent among your own people shall lift themselves up in order to fulfill the vision, but they shall fail.

15 Then the king of the north shall come and throw up siegeworks and take a well-fortified city. And the forces of the south shall not stand, or even his best troops, for there shall be no strength to stand.

16 But he who comes against him shall do as he wills, and none shall stand before him. And he shall stand in the glorious land, with destruction in his hand.

17 He shall set his face to come with the strength of his whole kingdom, and he shall bring terms of an agreement and perform them. He shall give him the daughter of women to destroy the kingdom, but it shall not stand or be to his advantage.

18 Afterward he shall turn his face to the coastlands and shall capture many of them, but a commander shall put an end to his insolence. Indeed, he shall turn his insolence back upon him.

19 Then he shall turn his face back toward the fortresses of his own land, but he shall stumble and fall, and shall not be found.

34 When they stumble, they shall receive a little help. And many shall join themselves to them with flattery,

35 and some of the wise shall stumble, so that they may be refined, purified, and made white, until the time of the end, for it still awaits the appointed time.

36 And the king shall do as he wills. He shall exalt himself and magnify himself above every god, and shall speak astonishing things against the God of gods. He shall prosper till the indignation is accomplished; for what is decreed shall be done.

37 He shall pay no attention to the gods of his fathers, or to the one beloved by women. He shall not pay attention to any other god, for he shall magnify himself above all.

38 He shall honor the god of fortresses instead of these. A god whom his fathers did not know he shall honor with gold and silver, with precious stones and costly gifts.

39 He shall deal with the strongest fortresses with the help of a foreign god. Those who acknowledge him he shall load with honor. He shall make them rulers over many and shall divide the land for a price.

Rome arises and attempts to destroy the prince of the covenant	End-Time Kingdoms arise and attempt to destroy the people of the covenant
20 Then shall arise in his place one who shall send an exactor of tribute for the glory of the kingdom. But within a few days he shall be broken, neither in anger nor in battle.	40 At the time of the end, the king of the south shall attack him, but the king of the north shall rush upon him like a whirlwind, with chariots and horsemen, and with many ships. And he shall come into countries and shall overflow and pass through.
21 In his place shall arise a contemptible person to whom royal majesty has not been given. He shall come in without warning and obtain the kingdom by flatteries.	41 He shall come into the glorious land. And tens of thousands shall fall, but these shall be delivered out of his hand: Edom and Moab and the main part of the Ammonites.
22 Armies shall be utterly swept away before him and broken, even the prince of the covenant.	42 He shall stretch out his hand against the countries, and the land of Egypt shall not escape.
	43 He shall become ruler of the treasures of gold and of silver, and all the precious things of Egypt, and the Libyans and the Cushites shall follow in his train.
	44 But news from the east and the north shall alarm him, and he shall go out with great fury to destroy and devote many to destruction.
	45 And he shall pitch his palatial tents between the sea and the glorious holy mountain. Yet he shall come to his end, with none to help him.

Note: The words *"burnt offering"* are crossed through. The translators supplied the words "burnt offering," which are not in the Hebrew text. In Hebrew, the word *regular* means "daily" or "continual" in connection with the sanctuary service. Hence, the passage suggests the power takes away the daily or continual sanctuary ministries and not the sacrifices themselves. Jesus was crucified under the reign of Imperial Rome, the Jewish temple had been destroyed, and no more sacrifices were needed as a substitution for sin.

With consistent, time-tested rules for our interpretation and principles to guide us, we will now move to our main focus of the longest of Daniel's prophecies found in chapter 11.

2: Ancient Persia, Daniel 11:2

And Daniel was there until the first year
of King Cyrus. —Daniel 1:24

Behold, three more kings shall arise in Persia, and
a fourth shall be far richer than all of them.
—Daniel 11:2

2. Medo-Persian Empire (539 - 331BC)

Daniel 2	Daniel 7	Daniel 8-9	Daniel 10-12
			Cyrus Delivers God's People

DANIEL WAS A faithful employee in the king's court for over seventy years. Babylon was already off the scene by 536 BC, and Daniel probably took retirement, being of considerable age. In Daniel chapter 10, we see him writing about his final vision. The vision of *"Great Conflicts"* was no ordinary vision. Soon after the *"third year of Cyrus king of Persia"* (Dan. 10:1), Daniel must have died, being over ninety-years-old, serving God first and man second.

In Daniel 2, we find Medo-Persia nearly as glorious and rich as its predecessor as silver is to gold, and in Daniel 7, a strong and ferocious bear, yet not as swift and skillful in battle as its predecessor, the lion. Daniel 8 and 9 reveals that Persia was very good to God's people, not only freeing them of Babylonian bondage but allowing them to rebuild the Temple with Persian finances and resources. Finally, in Daniel 11, we see the beginning of the downfall of Persia to the rising Greek kingdom on their western front.

Daniel 11 only gives one verse to this powerful kingdom.

> *And now I will show you the truth. Behold, three more kings shall arise in Persia, and a fourth shall be far richer than all of them. And when he has become strong through his riches, he shall stir up all against the kingdom of Greece.* (Dan. 11:2)

Persian Political History

Babylon's Defeat

Babylon fell by a two-pronged attack. King Cyrus led his army through the Babylonian cities of Opis and Sipper, and then General Ugbaru/Gubaru attacked Babylon itself.

We read in the Nabonidus Chronicle:

> *When Cyrus did battle at Opis on the [bank of] the Tigris against the army of Akkad, the people of Akkad retreated.*

He carried off the plunder (and) slaughtered the people. On the fourteenth day Sippar was captured without a battle. Nabonidus fled. On the sixteenth day, Ugbaru, governor of Gutium, and the army of Cyrus, without battle they entered Babylon. Afterwards, after Nabonidus retreated, he was captured in Babylon. Until the end of the month, the shield-(bearing troops) from Gutium surrounded the gates of Esagil...On the third day of the month Arahsamna, Cyrus entered Babylon. The harû-vessels were filled before him. There was peace in the city while Cyrus, (his) greeting to Babylon in its entirety spoke. Gubaru, his district officer, appointed the district officers in Babylon.[3]

Nabonidus Chronicle

---

[3] https://www.livius.org/sources/content/mesopotamian-chronicles-content/abc-7-nabonidus-chronicle/

You can read the Biblical narrative regarding the fall of the city in Daniel 5,

The Four "Kings," of Persia

And now I will show you the truth. Behold, three more kings shall arise in Persia, and a fourth shall be far richer than all of them. (Dan. 11:2a)

As the king of Persia, Cyrus had already been identified in Daniel 10:1. The three kings to follow were (1) Cambyses II, Cyrus's older son, (2) Bardiya (or Smerdis) Cyrus's younger son, who only reigned less than a year and is generally left out of the records of Achaemenid kings, and (3) Darius I, the Great, son of Hystaspes, a Persian satrap or governor. The fourth king was Xerxes I, the same as Ahasuerus in the book of Esther.

What is significant about the prophecy of *"great conflicts"* in Daniel 11 is that each kingdom rises until the next kingdom checkmates its power and conquest. The Persian Empire lasted from the fall of Babylon in 539 BC until the conquest of Greece by Alexander in 333 BC. Yet, in Daniel 11, Persia ends when Greece breaks its conquest and expansion with the Persian defeats in battles at Peloponnese, Plataea, and Mycale by the smaller, less equipped, and fragmented Greek military alliance in 480 BC.

Medo-Persian Rulers

Cyrus II "the Great" 550–529 BC (Conquered Babylon and Lydia)

Cambyses II 529–522 BC (Conquered Egypt)

Darius I 522–486 BC (King of Persians and Medes)

Xerxes I 486–465 BC (Lost against the Greeks; Husband of Queen Esther)

————Persian Dominance ends in Daniel 11:3————

Artaxerxes I 465–425 BC (Decree to rebuild Jerusalem)

Xerxes II 425–424 BC

Darius II 423–404 BC

Artaxerxes II 404–359 BC

Artaxerxes III 358–338 BC

Artaxerxes IV 338–336 BC

Darius III 336–330 BC (Lost the kingdom to Alexander the Great)

Artaxerxes V 330–329 BC (Killed by Alexander)

The "far richer" king

> *And when he has become strong through his riches...*
> (Dan. 11:2b).

Let us back up to this "far richer" king. His wealth and extravagance of Xerxes I, or King Ahasuerus, can be easily seen in the first passage of Esther 1.

> *Now in the days of Ahasuerus, the Ahasuerus who reigned from India to Ethiopia over 127 provinces, in those days when King Ahasuerus sat on his royal throne in Susa, the citadel, in the third year of his reign he gave a feast for all his officials and servants. The army of Persia and Media and the nobles and governors of the provinces were before him, while he showed the riches of his royal glory and the splendor and pomp of his greatness for many days, 180 days. And when these days were completed, the king gave for all the people present in Susa the citadel, both great and small, a feast lasting for seven days in the court of the garden of the king's palace. There were white cotton curtains and violet hangings fastened with cords of fine linen and purple to silver rods and marble pillars, and also couches of gold and silver on a mosaic pavement of porphyry, marble, mother-of-pearl, and precious stones. Drinks were served in golden vessels, vessels of different kinds, and the royal wine was lavished according to the bounty of the king. And drinking was according to this edict: "There is no compulsion." For the king had given orders to all the staff of his palace to do as each man desired. (Est. 1:1–8)*

Fight against "Greece"

> *[H]e shall stir up all against the kingdom of Greece.* (Dan. 11:2c)

In 499 BC, the Ionian Revolt against the Persian Empire began on the westernmost section of Asia Minor. King Darius the Great started to take measures to quell the uprisings and conquer the Greek peninsula. His generals in the field were victorious at Thrace and Macedon in the north. The Greeks halted Darius's expansion at the famous Battle of Marathon. While technically won by Persia, the smaller Greek army proved to be a force to be reckoned with, and Athens was saved from invasion. Darius was making plans for the invasion of Greece when he fell ill and died in 486 BC.

His successor, King Xerxes I, raised a vast army and navy from forty different nations, and in 480 BC, marched into Greece with himself at the head. Initially, Xerxes was successful in getting allegiance from the northern regions of the Greek peninsula. As the Persians marched through areas, they would send out their envoys ahead to the cities demanding "earth and water," symbolizing the cities alliance to Persian rule in exchange for not being attacked, captured, and plundered. Just the sight of the vastness of the Persian army would compel most cities to capitulate. However, Athens was not given this opportunity presumably because it and Sparta had scorned the envoys Darius had sent just a few years earlier. Herodotus records that Spartans threw the envoy into a well, and the Athenians cast their envoys into a gorge with the message "Dig it out for yourselves!"

Xerxes fought in the Battle of Thermopylae in 480 BC. The Persians gained control of Phocis, Boeotia, and Attica. Yet, the simultaneous naval battle of Artemisium was essentially a stalemate. The way to Plataea, Thespiae, and Athens was now open to Xerxes, and he pillaged and razed them to the ground.

At this point, secular historians would say that fate turned on Xerxes, but for Bible believers, we would say the hand of God intervened. At the naval Battle of Salamis in 480 BC, Xerxes's Persian forces were turned back at Peloponnese by the vastly outnumbered Greek navy.

The final land battle occurred near Plataea in 479 BC. Here, even with the Persians vastly outnumbering the Greek's alliance, the Greeks managed to outmaneuver their foes. Persian losses were 30,000, while the Greeks lost only 2,000. Xerxes now lost control of the eastern peninsula of Attica and Boeotia near the center of Greece.

Simultaneously, the naval Battle of Mycale took place where the Greek navy bested the Persia navy. Xerxes lost control over all the Aegean islands between Asia Minor and the Greek peninsula.

Over the next few years, the Greek city-states expelled the Persian overlords, and by 465 BC, the Persians had lost all territories on the Greek Peninsula, and all desired to retake the region. And the prophecy stands true, *"he shall stir up all against the kingdom of Greece."*

Two Deliverers—Cyrus and Michael

King Cyrus was the great deliverer who freed the Jews from Babylonian captivity. In Daniel 12:1, we see Michael delivering God's people from the great time of trouble in the last days. Cyrus and Michael are parallel deliverers each in their time. Of King Cyrus, we read:

> *Thus says the Lord, your Redeemer...who says of Cyrus, 'He is my shepherd, and he shall fulfill all my purpose'; saying of Jerusalem, 'She shall be built,' and of the Temple, 'Your foundation shall be laid.'" Thus says the Lord to his anointed, to Cyrus, whose right hand I have grasped, to subdue nations before him and to loose the belts of kings, to open doors before him that gates may not be closed.* (Isa. 44:28–45:1)

Of Michael, we read:

> *At that time shall arise Michael, the great prince who has charge of your people. And there shall be a time of trouble, such as never has been since there was a nation till that time. But at that time your people shall be delivered, everyone whose name shall be found written in the book.* (Dan. 12:1)

After freeing the Jews, King Cyrus allowed for the establishment of worship in Jerusalem and instituting a time of peace. Similarly, yet with more power and amazement, Prince Michael will deliver God's end-time people, establish genuine worship in the New Jerusalem, and create an everlasting time of peace.

3: Ancient Greece and Hellenism

Then the king of the north shall...And the forces of the south shall not stand. —Daniel 11:15

3. Greek Empire (331 - 31BC)

Daniel 2	Daniel 7	Daniel 8-9	Daniel 10-12
			**KON - Seleucid Dynasty** **KOS - Ptolemaic Dynasty**

THE PROPHECIES OF Greece in Daniel 2, 7, and 8 follow the same pattern as the former kingdoms, describing characteristics and actions perpetrated by the empire. Yet this is not the case for Daniel 9 and 11. While Daniel 9 has scant information during this period, Daniel 11 has enormous prophetic data on the Greek Hellenistic period. One might ask, "Why in Daniel 11 is all this information given on Greece when there is little about this time in Daniel 9?" and "How does that affect us today?" The answer lies in the purpose of Daniel 11. The angel tells Daniel this prophecy is about *"what will happen to your people in the latter days"* (Dan. 10:14). Hence, this long narrative about great conflicts (Dan. 10:1) between the kings of the

North and South in Daniel 11 is essential since it has a message for us, God's people, in the end-times.

In Daniel 2, Greece is practically a mediocre empire with bronze trailing in value to gold and silver and not as robust as iron. In Daniel 7, we see swift and complete conquest like a leopard with four wings. In Daniel 8, we again encounter swiftness, but this time as a goat with the defeat of adversaries. Then we see the four divisions coming up only after the initial unity thrust has taken place. Finally, in Daniel 11, we can see Daniel 7 and 8 interpreted through the actions of a mighty king and the disunion of his kingdom after his death. But Daniel 11 continues with the conflict of the kings of the North and South.

Greece and Hellenistic Political History

The Leopard, the Shaggy Goat, and the Mighty King

There are very few things with near-universal agreement regarding anything in the Bible, but this may be one of those very few cases. Alexander the Great of Macedon, was the leopard of Daniel 7, the shaggy goat of Daniel 8, and the mighty king of Daniel 11:3.

A "male goat came from the west."(Dan. 8:5)

Alexander the Great received the kingdom of Macedonia after his father, Phillip II of Macedon, was assassinated by his bodyguard in 336 BC. Phillip had planned to unite the Greek city-states and march on Persia. Alexander, who was previously under the tutelage of Aristotle, ascended to the throne at age twenty-one. After securing his throne from rivals, he set out to take the Balkans and put down revolts to his authority. With all Greece secure by 335 BC, Alexander next crossed the Hellespont, or the Strait of Gallipoli, into Asia Minor and Persia in 334 BC. It is reported, he threw a spear into the ground in Asia Minor and pronounced that he accepted Persia as a gift from the gods.

334 BC Battle of Granicus River

The Persian governors in Asia Minor combined their forces and met Alexander at the Granicus River in Asia Minor. Alexander, with his cavalry, charged across the river on the right and left flank to start the battle, then the Greek phalanxes moved across the river in the center. The fighting was intense, and in the melee, Alexander was saved from sure death by the quick response of one of his officers, Cleitus the Black. As the Persian cavalry soldier was bringing his arm forward to strike the mortal blow to Alexander, Cleitus sliced the soldier's arm off, saving the young king and preserving the prophecies of Daniel. A hole suddenly opened in the Persia line. Immediately, the Greek infantry moved forward, separating the Persian right flank from the center. As the Greek infantry advanced into the Persian line's rear, the Persian flanks retreated, and the phalanxes enveloped the center. Hence, Alexander had won the first of three main battles with the Persians.

Alexander consolidated his forces and moved through Asia Minor with relative ease, capturing the region's capital at Sardis. With few exceptions, the captured cities were allowed to remain autonomous and democratic. At the city of Gordium, the famed Gordian Knot was shown to Alexander. An ancient oracle prophesied that whoever could "undo" the knot would be "King of Asia." Sources vary as to if Alexander pulled out his sword and sliced the knot into two halves, or if he pulled out lynchpins from the yoke holding the two ends of the knot, then untying it with ease. Either way, he was able to undo the knot fulfilling the prophecy. Yet, in reality, it was not because of this pagan prophecy that he went forth to conquer Asia. We know it was the prophecies of Daniel who forecasted God's will for Alexander over 200 years before.

333 BC Battle of Issus

Obviously, the Persians were not going to let Alexander gobble up their vast kingdom. Upon hearing of the defeat of his army in Asia Minor, King Darius III set out with a massive force to end Alexander's intrusion into his realm. Alexander marched his troops near the Mediterranean Sea, anticipated Darius would fight in the open plain, and headed for the plane near the city of Issus separating Asia Minor and Syria. However, Darius's forces traversed through the narrow passes and were finally discovered behind Alexander's rear. After hastily shifting his 40,000 plus troops to meet his foe, taking up positions to his rear, Alexander stationed his forces again with the phalanxes in the center and cavalry of the flanks. Darius's overwhelming force is estimated upwards of 60,000 by modern historians and over 250,000 by ancient sources. Because of the small coastal plain with mountains on the opposite side, Darius had a double line of troops.

The Persian cavalry crossed the river first, and intensive fighting erupted between the two forces. Alexander sent his center phalanxes with their long spears forward under immense rain of Persian arrows and projectiles. Yet, they made it across the river as Alexander led the cavalry on the opposite side across the river. While the fighting was fierce, Alexander's charge broke the Persian flank, and the Greek cavalry turned inward to relieve the besieged Greek phalanxes troops in the center. At this point, the Persian rear including Darius's command post were defenseless, hence Alexander charged, putting Darius to flight. While Alexander's forces won the battle in the center and right flank, the Persian cavalry continued crushing his left flank. Alexander broke off his pursuit of Darius and swung his cavalry behind the Persians to envelope them. Nevertheless, the Persian troops also turned and fled, seeing Alexander's soldiers all around them and learning of Darius's cowardly flight from the battle.

The defeat was a total conquest of the Persian forces, including up to 40,000 of them killed or wounded, five generals killed in action, Darius fleeing the field, and the capture of Darius's wife, mother, and two daughters, one of which, Stateira II, Alexander would later marry. It was the first defeat ever of the Persian army with King Darius at its head.

Battle of Issus as depicted in the Alexander Mosaic, House of the Faun, Pompeii

332 BC Siege of Tyre

The Persians had a significant naval fleet in the Mediterranean Sea, but Alexander had no navy to confront them. Instead, he took the seaport cities to prevent the fleet from being resupplied. This practice worked well with little resistance until he reached Tyre. The city, containing two harbors on the mainland and an island with high walls right up to the sea, was a strategic Persian naval port. Alexander spent seven months of his campaign besieging and building a causeway of nearly one kilometer or over 1,000 yards to the city. Alexander's causeway forever changed the city. Today, there is no longer an island but instead a peninsula with a land bridge to the city.

With the capture of the city, Alexander did something he rarely did. He killed and crucified a significant number of the defenders and took 30,000 inhabitants to be slaves. Why were the Tyrians so stubborn, and why was Alexander so harsh? Some would say he was mad because they resisted and cost him a seven-month delay. Or maybe he wanted to make an example as to what happens to people who resist him. There is another answer... because the Bible said so. The prophet Isaiah, some 400 years before this incident, gave this oracle about Tyre:

> *The oracle concerning Tyre. Wail, O ships of Tarshish, for Tyre is laid waste, without house or harbor!*
>
> *Now the coastlands tremble on the day of your fall, and the coastlands that are on the sea are dismayed at your passing.* (Isa. 23:1)

Tyre was Alexander's last port siege, and the other seaport cities capitulated without a fight. The Persian fleet now had no port. After a short siege at Gaza, Alexander entered Egypt without a fight. He was treated as a liberator and declared the son of the god Amun. Here he founded Alexandria, which would become prominent for its culture and library under the Ptolemaic dynasty.

The Greek historians never discuss Alexander's entrance into Jerusalem. It would seem unlikely he took Jerusalem on his initial march down the coast because of his objective to deprive the Persian fleet of port access. Since he had already conquered the cities along the coast road, and it is more probable that coming back through Palestine, he took the inner road going through Jerusalem. Josephus states that the priests went out to meet Alexander and showed him the portions in Daniel which spoke of his conquest.

Just imagine the High Priest in his royal purple robe reading from the scroll of Daniel 8, with Alexander intently listening.

> *As I (Daniel) was considering, behold, a male goat came from the west across the face of the whole earth, without touching the ground. And the goat had a conspicuous horn between his eyes. He came to the ram with the two horns, which I had seen standing on the bank of the canal, and he ran at him in his powerful wrath. I saw him come close to the ram, and he was enraged against him and struck the ram and broke his two horns. And the ram had no power to stand before him, but he cast him down to the ground and trampled on him. And there was no one who could rescue the ram from his power. Then the goat became exceedingly great, but when he was strong, the great horn was broken, and instead of it there came up four conspicuous horns toward the four winds of heaven.* (Dan. 8:5–8)

> *As for the ram that you saw with the two horns, these are the kings of Media and Persia. And the (shaggy) goat is the king of Greece. And the great horn between his eyes is the first king.* (Dan. 8:20, 22)

Whether or not this happened, Alexander did allow the Jews to continue their temple services and gave autonomy to the city.

331 BC Battle of Gaugamela

Darius returned to Babylon to reorganize his army and recruit many troops from his numerous provinces. Alexander had replaced his slain troops and bolstered his force from captured territories to just under 50,000, yet the Persians still outnumbered them with estimates well over 60,000 up to one million.

Darius chose a large flat plain in northern Mesopotamia to spread his massive forces and allow for a relatively smooth surface for his 200 chariots and 15 war elephants. He moved up his cavalry on both flanks and the chariots on the right forward to initiate the battle. This maneuver caused a hole in the Persian line on the right side, which Alexander immediately exploited, and he found himself heading straight for Darius's position. However, at the same time, a hole developed in the left of the Greek frontline. The chariots on the left side moved forward to enter and exploit the gap. Instead of battling with the charioteers with their eighteen-foot spears, the front phalanx line opened wider and let the chariots come straight through the phalanx line. The charioteers ended up with the rear line of Greek infantry with their shorter swords used for close combat to their front while the front line of phalanxes closed ranks, enveloping the chariots. Alexander's infantry on the flanks, although outnumbered, held their ground during the battle. With the chariots out of action and Alexander's cavalry behind the Persian center line charging for the command post, Darius fled the battlefield again. Seeing what was happening, his forces cut off the engagement and also absconded the scene.

Alexander captured the entire Persian baggage train containing much wealth, and then he headed to Babylon, Susa, and Persepolis. Several more small engagements took place, and Darius was finally cornered and assassinated by one of his satraps in Bactria. However, Alexander's soldiers revolted after conquering territory up to the Indus River, forcing him to return back towards the west.

Making his capital in Babylon, Alexander began to rebuild the city. Historians would say fortune turned against him, but we know God was about to fulfill prophecy. After a short reign, he either fell sick of malaria, alcohol poisoning, or a combination of the two fulfilling the prophecies *"as soon as he has arisen," "the great horn was broken."* He was dead at age thirty-three in the year 323 BC. It is reported that on his deathbed, they asked Alexander who the kingdom should go to. His reply was, "to the strongest."

"four wings of a bird" (Dan. 7:6) and *"four conspicuous horns"* (Dan. 8:8)

The "strongest," including many of Alexander's generals, would vie to control either particular areas or the entire empire. The Partition of Babylon distributed regional satrapies across the empire was established with Philip III, Alexander's half-brother administering the empire until Alexander's unborn child by Roxana was of governing age. This agreement soon after fell apart.

Four of Alexander's generals, Craterus, Perdiccas, Antipater, and Nearchus, would die or be killed in various battles between 321–312 BC. Philip III was executed in 317 by Olympias, and Alexander's son, Alexander IV, with his mother, Roxana, were both killed on Cassander's orders in 310 BC.

The following chart summarizes the results of the four Wars of the Diadochi after Alexander's death in 223 BC.

Date	War	Victors	Losers
322–319 BC	*First War of the Diadochi*	Antipater, Ptolemy Craterus (killed) Antigonus	Antigenes, Seleucus Perdiccas (executed)
318–315 BC	*Second War of the Diadochi*	Antigonus, Cassander Seleucus, Ptolemy, Lysimachus, Demetrius (Antigonus's son) Phillip III (Alexander's half-brother, executed)	Polyperchon, Peucestas, Eumenes (executed) Eudemus (executed) Antigenes (executed) Olympias (Alexander's mother, executed)
314–311 BC	*Third War of the Diadochi*	Ended in a compromise with five kingdoms governed by Ptolemy, Seleucus, Cassander, Lysimachus, Antigonus	
308–301 BC	*Fourth War of the Diadochi, (Battle of Ipsus, 301)*	Ptolemy, Seleucus, Cassander, Lysimachus,	Antigonus (killed), Demetrius

For over twenty years, there was a power struggle in the empire. The "four wings of a bird" and "four conspicuous horns" were what remained, and with the death of Alexander IV, the kingdom did not go "to his posterity."

The Diadochi kingdoms and their neighbors
after the Battle of Ipsos 301 BC

With the Battle of Ipsus concluded, Cassander took control of Macedonia and Greece regions or the Western section. General Lysimachus took control of Thrace and Asia Minor regions in the North. General Seleucus I took Mesopotamian land, Persian land, and the area to the Indus River in the East. Finally, General Ptolemy I, took Egypt, Cyprus, and the southern Asia Minor regions.

The Kings of the North and South

Even though there was a specific ruling party in each region, the situation did not last long. Lysimachus in Thrace and Asia Minor lost his kingdom to Seleucus in 281 BC at the Battle of Corupedium.

Shortly after Cassander's death, a power struggle emerged in Macedon with one party after the next seizing power. Eventually,

Macedon was ruled by the Antigonid dynasty, ruling over Macedon and some cities in Greece until Rome defeated them in 168 BC at the Battle of Pydna, thus ending the Macedonian division of Alexander's empire. Additionally, many see the Battle of Corinth in 146 BC as the final battle of Greek resistance to Rome on the peninsula.

In Selucia, the Romans defeated Antiochus III in Asia Minor in 188 BC, and they became a vassal kingdom of Rome. The final stage was in 64 BC when Roman General Pompey took all the territory in Syria, and Antiochus XIII (Asiaticus) was deposed and killed. Syria was from then a Roman province.

Ptolemy's kingdom was relatively stable but weak militarily. In the mid-190's BC, their southern Asia Minor regions were conquered by Seleucia. The Romans subsequently repelled the Seleucids from the region but refused to give back the Polemic holdings on the southern coast of Asia Minor. Hence, while never openly defeated by Rome, the Ptolemies in Egypt were under the thumb of the Roman Republic by 188 BC. Ptolemaic Egypt lasted until AD 31. During the Roman Civil War, Queen Cleopatra VII, the final official ruler of Egypt, was defeated at the Battle of Actium. Egypt became a Roman province at that time.

In Daniel 11, during the Greek Hellenistic period, we first see the kings of the South in control, and then the kings of the North seem to take over. Two powers are struggling here. Remember back in Daniel 2, and the belly and thighs of bronze? The belly of the image could be analogous to the united Greek empire of Alexander in the belly and then the divided Greek Hellenic period in the thighs. The two thighs in Daniel 2 and Daniel 11 can be seen as the two kingdoms of the Ptolemies and the Seleucids, battling during this period. Why just these two kingdoms? Why not Cassander's kingdom or the approaching Roman Republic? While Daniel 2 and 7 give us glimpses of the political affairs of nations, Daniel 8, 9, and 11 tell us what was happening to God's people and those centered around Jerusalem. Only the Ptolemies in Egypt and the Seleucids east of the Euphrates had any real impact on the Jewish nation and could affect the temple practices. These two kingdoms would fight each other in Palestine to increase or defend their territory from 301 BC to 163 BC.

Regarding the conflicts between the Ptolemies and Seleucids, the Palestine Historian Chester Starr has observed,

> *If there were six Syrian wars between the Ptolemies and Seleucids(,) the causes were in part personal pride and desire for glory, but also the advantages to be gained from controlling the Mediterranean ports to which the luxuries of India and Arabia largely flowed.*

> *"And after some years he* (King of the South from v. 11) *shall come on with a great army and abundant supplies"*(Dan. 11:13)

While the Ptolemies in Egypt were a robust and stable kingdom through the third and middle of the second century, the empire began to decline by the last quarter. Wallace (1938), in *Census and Poll-Tax in Ptolemaic Egypt*, gives great insight into this period and, specifically, Ptolemy IV Philopator.

Ptolemy's father had died of disease and left the throne to his son, Ptolemy IV. Within a few years, he was again going to war with the Seleucids under Antiochus III.

Daniel 11 depicts the acts of the kings of the Ptolemies and the Seleucia from 301 BC to 163 BC. The chart below shows these kings during this period with the specific kings mentioned in Daniel 11:5–19 highlighted.

Ptolemaic Dynasty KOS	Dates	Seleucid Dynasty KON
Ptolemy I Soter (rule over Jerusalem began in 301BC)	306–282 BC	
	305–281 BC	Seleukos I Nikator
Ptolemy II Philadelphos	284–246 BC	
	281–261 BC	Antiochus I Soter
	261–246 BC	Antiochus II Theos
	246–226 BC	Seleukos II Kallinikos
Ptolemy III Euergetes	246–222 BC	
	226–223 BC	Seleukos III
	223–187 BC	Antiochus III Megas (rule over Jerusalem began in 201BC)
Ptolemy IV Philopator (rule over Jerusalem ended 201 BC)	222–204 BC	
Ptolemy V Epiphanes	210–180 BC	
	187–175 BC	Seleukos IV Philopator
	175–164 BC	Antiochus IV Epiphanes (rule over Jerusalem ended in 163 BC)

The Battle of Raphia

The Battle of Raphia occurred in 217 BC near Gaza, and at stake was control over Syria and Palestine, and if Ptolemy was defeated, possibly even Egypt. While Ptolemy had an advantage in the infantry, Antiochus had more elephants to engage in battle. Both sides moved their elephants in first, with the Indian elephants of Antiochus pushing the smaller African elephants back. Polybius describes the elephants fighting:

> Ptolemy's elephants came to close quarters with the foe: seated on these, the soldiers in the howdahs maintained a brilliant fight, lunging at and striking each other with crossed pikes. But the elephants themselves fought still more brilliantly, using all their strength in the encounter, and pushing against each other, forehead to forehead.

> The way in which elephants fight is this: they get their tusks entangled and jammed, and then push against one another with all their might, trying to make each other yield ground until one of them proving superior in strength has pushed aside the other's trunk; and when once he can get a side blow at his enemy, he pierces him with his tusks as a bull would with his horns[4].

The phalanx soldiers moved forward, and because of the superior forces of the Egyptians, the Seleucid phalanxes were starting to be pushed back. Ptolemy, himself, was in the mists of the center

---

[4] http://www.perseus.tufts.edu/hopper/text?doc=Perseus%3Atext%3A1999.01.0234%3Abook%3D5%3Achapter%3D84

exhorting his phalanx soldiers on. At the same time, Ptolemy's cavalry was routing the Seleucids on the right side. Antiochus, jubilantly looking at the left side of the battle, believed he was winning the day, but then he realized too late the right was getting routed, and his center phalanx soldiers were being driven back in mass. Antiochus attempted to regroup, but the Seleucid retreat was too immense, and they fled the field.

> *"In those times many shall rise against the king of the south"*
> (Dan. 11:14a)

Ptolemy IV goes home triumphant, but on the home front, he begins having problems. Wallace (1938) believes Ptolemy IV implemented census and poll-tax, which included Jerusalem in the 206–205 BC census. The Jews, having been used to their sovereignty, undoubtedly resented this move. Yet, this is a political move and appears in no way to affect the temple services. During this time, Ptolemy also had several revolts in his kingdom from native Egyptians, dissatisfaction with the Egyptian priesthood, and political murders. All these constituted a "rise against the King of the South."

> The Jews, as we know from III Maccabees, looked back upon the reign of Philopator as one of oppression and injustice, and they took their peculiar revenge by blackening his memory. The revolts of the Egyptians which began in his reign and were not finally suppressed until some years after his successor came to the throne are an adequate testimonial to the feeling of his native subjects towards Philopator. (Wallace, 1938, p. 420)

Mixing Religion and State, Tax Farming, and Rebellion in Jerusalem

> *Also, violent men of your people shall exalt themselves in fulfillment of the vision, but they shall fall.* (Dan. 11:14b)

This seemingly trivial verse is anything but trivial. Recall that after the Babylonian exile, God sent decrees, messages, and prophets to reestablish the sacrifices on the altar, the sanctuary service, and the city with its economy. There was never a command to reestablish a national independent Jewish state. Yet, this is what many in Hellenistic Jerusalem attempted. Add also that the high priest now assumed the role of a political ruler and often a general. Before the Babylonian captivity, Judah, while a theocratic state, maintained the separation of religious and political power by a succession of Davidic kingship and Levitical priesthood. David refused to fight Absalom in Jerusalem, and God intervened. Again, we find God stopping David from building the temple because he had blood on his hands. We also have the narrative of King Uzziah.

> *But when he (Uzziah) was strong, he grew proud, to his destruction. For he was unfaithful to the Lord his God and entered the temple of the Lord to burn incense on the altar of incense. But Azariah the priest went in after him, with eighty priests of the Lord who were men of valor, and they withstood King Uzziah and said to him,*
>
> *"It is not for you, Uzziah, to burn incense to the Lord, but for the priests, the sons of Aaron, who are consecrated to burn incense. Go out of the sanctuary, for you have done wrong,*

and it will bring you no honor from the Lord God." Then Uzziah was angry. *Now he had a censer in his hand to burn incense, and when he became angry with the priests, leprosy[a] broke out on his forehead in the presence of the priests in the house of the Lord, by the altar of incense. And Azariah the chief priest and all the priests looked at him, and behold, he was leprous in his forehead! And they rushed him out quickly, and he himself hurried to go out, because the Lord had struck him. And King Uzziah was a leper to the day of his death, and being a leper lived in a separate house, for he was excluded from the house of the Lord.* (2 Chron. 26:16–21)

Not only was the mixing of political and religious authority at issue, taxation and census taking were also going to lead to tension with both the Ptolemies and the Seleucids. Ptolemy III added the Jews to the great census in 206–205 BC and subsequently taxed the land, which the Jews noticeably resented. The result of this was the desire of the Jewish leaders to revolt and join the Seleucid kingdom. Wallace (1938) sheds light on this subject.

> The writer of Ecclesiastes, according to Barton, describes the conditions in Palestine at the end of Philopator's reign: "Then I returned and saw all the that are done under the sun: and behold the tears of such as were oppressed, and they had no comforter; and on the side of their oppressors there was power, but they had no comforter. Wherefore I praised the dead..." That the oppressions were those of taxation will become evident. The spies of Ptolemy are probably referred to in

Ecclesiastes, X, 20: " Curse not the king, no, not in thy thought; and curse not the rich in thy bedchamber; for a bird of the air shall carry thy voice, and that which hath wings shall tell the matter." Despite the writer's feeling expressed in these metaphors Ptolemy had not enough spies in Palestine. The negotiations of the Jews with Antiochus continued and encouraged him to carry on in spite of the early defeats of his army in Coele-Syria at the hands of the Ptolemaic general Scopas, and to complete the conquest of that province by the bloody battle of Panion, the successful siege of Sidon and the capture of Batanaea, Abila, Gadara, and Jerusalem. Jerusalem voluntarily opened its gates to Antiochus. The reason for this sudden reversal of a Jewish policy that had begun with the reign of Ptolemy I Soter is not hard to find. Josephus quotes a letter of instructions, alleged to have been sent by Antiochus to Ptolemaeus (his general in charge of the newly acquired province of Palestine), which indirectly reveals the terms upon which the Jews agreed to surrender to Antiochus. I hold no brief for the authenticity of the letter, but I believe that it represents the facts quite accurately. The significant portion reads as follows: "And let the elders and the priests and the scribes of the temple and the singers in the temple be freed from capitation taxes and from the crown-tribute and other tribute. In order, too, that the city (Jerusalem) may recover its inhabitants, I grant to those who now inhabit it and to those who move into it up to the month of Hyperberetaeus to be tax-free for three years. Thereafter I remit to them a third part of the taxes so that they may recover from the harm done them." The remission of taxes must have been the inducement that drew the Jews away from their old loyalty to Egypt. The death of Philopator in 204 or 203 B.C. and the accession of Epiphanes, while still a child, gave Antiochus his opportunity to take advantage of the disaffection of the Jews, and by 198 B. C. Coele-Syria was forever lost to the Ptolemies. (Wallace, 1938, p 439)

Both the Ptolemies and Seleucids enlisted members of the Jewish community to collect the taxes. A tax farmer is someone who pays the required revenue for a particular region to the governor and then taxes the people to recuperate his losses. From 220 to 198 BC, Joseph ben Tobiah and his son, Hyrcanus, gained immense wealth from tax farming. Josephus gives an account of the high priest Onias II refusing to pay taxes to Ptolemy III ca 242 BC. Interestingly, the phrase *"the violent among your own people"* is translated as the *"robbers of thy people"* in the KJV. It seems reasonable that the "robbers" during the Hellenistic period could be tax farmers, much like Levi Matthew and Zacchaeus before meeting Jesus during the Roman years.

We can see the *"violent among your own people"* as Jews who mixed religious and political power in a single person and committed aggressive acts against census-taking and taxation, beginning with Ptolemy III. Moreover, they constructed a "vision" for an independent state of Judah. Yet, the calamities that befell the Hellenistic Jews due to these revolts and the plain statement that the vision "shall fail" is a good indication that God was not with them in this.

From the words of Moses, we learn God's vision for the nation of Israel:

And if you faithfully obey the voice of the Lord your God, being careful to do all his commandments that I command you today, the Lord your God will set you high above all the nations of the earth. And all these blessings shall come upon you and overtake you, if you obey the voice of the Lord your God Blessed shall you be in the city, and blessed shall you be in the field. Blessed shall be the fruit of your womb and the fruit of your ground and the fruit of your cattle, the increase of your herds and the young of your flock. Blessed shall be your basket and your kneading bowl. Blessed shall you be when you come in, and blessed shall you be when you go out.

The Lord will cause your enemies who rise against you to be defeated before you. They shall come out against you one way and flee before you seven ways. The Lord will command the blessing on you in your barns and in all that you undertake. And he will bless you in the land that the Lord your God is giving you. The Lord will establish you as a people holy to himself, as he has sworn to you, if you keep the commandments of the Lord your God and walk in his ways. And all the peoples of the earth shall see that you are called by the name of the Lord, and they shall be afraid of you. And the Lord will make you abound in prosperity, in the fruit of your womb and in the fruit of your livestock and in the fruit of your ground, within the land that the Lord swore to your fathers to give you. The Lord will open to you his good treasury, the heavens, to give the rain to your land in its season and to bless all the work of your hands. And you shall lend to many nations, but you shall not borrow. And the Lord will make you the head and not the tail, and you shall only go up and not down, if you obey the commandments of the Lord your God, which I command you today, being careful to do them, and if you do not turn aside from any of the words that I command you today, to the right hand or to the left, to go after other gods to serve them. (Deut. 28:1–14)

Even with this and many other great promises like it, Israelites went their own way and created their own vision spilling their blood and the blood of their children. This lamentable scene is repeated time and time again, all because they would not heed the words of the Psalmist: *"Wait on the Lord; be strong, and let your heart take courage; wait for the Lord"* (Ps. 27:14).

Without God's divine protection, the next 300 years were horrific for the renegade Jewish nation. While Antiochus III, the Great, *"stood"* in Jerusalem, he never employed that *"destruction in his hand"* (Dan. 11:16). This was left to his son, Antiochus IV Epiphanes, who suspended the Jewish sanctuary service in 167–164 BC and attempted to Hellenize the kingdom. He built an altar to Zeus and sacrificed swine on it.

Josephus records the following about Antiochus:

> Now Antiochus was not satisfied either with his unexpected taking the city (Jerusalem), or with its pillage, or with the great slaughter he had made there; but being overcome with his violent passions, and remembering what he had suffered during the siege, he compelled the Jews to dissolve the laws of their country,

and to keep their infants uncircumcised, and to sacrifice swine's flesh upon the altar; against which they all opposed themselves, and the most approved among them were put to death. (Flavius Josephus, *The War of the Jews*, Book 1.1 §2)

These stringent policies resulted in the Maccabean revolt, and in a series of battles between 167 and 161 BC, the Seleucids were continually beaten and eventually driven from Palestine. For the most part, Jerusalem and its surroundings were a free and independent state, albeit with much warring and bloodshed.

What about Antiochus IV Epiphanes?

Many in the Christian community feel Antiochus IV Epiphanes fulfilled the prophecies of the little horn of Daniel 7 and 8 and was one of the Kings of the North in Daniel 11. Below are five reasons why he cannot be the Little Horn or the King of the North.

1. In Daniel 2, the nation after Greece was Rome, and the prophecies in 7, 8–9, and 10–11 have parallel kingdoms with chapter 2.

2. In chapter 7, the Little Horn came up out of the ten, therefore the eleventh horn. Antiochus was, in reality, the 8th king of the Greek Seleucid kingdom, not the eleventh.

3. In chapter 8, Medo-Persia was "great"(v. 4), Greece was "very great" (v. 8), and the next kingdom was "exceedingly great" (v. 9), yet Antiochus inherited his kingdom from his father. He was stopped from expanding his *inherited* empire into Egypt by a Roman Counsel in 168 BC. His kingdom, thus, never became "exceedingly great," as stated in the prophecy. Interesting is the departure of Antiochus IV from his attempted invasion of Egypt. Gaius Popillius Laenas was the Roman Republic consul in Egypt at the time, and the following is reported regarding his incident:

> Popilius, stern and imperious as ever, drew a circle around the king with the stick he carried and said, "Before you step out of that circle give me a reply to lay before the senate." For a few moments he hesitated, astounded at such a peremptory order, and at last replied, "I will do what the senate thinks right."[5]

With his defeat in Egypt, the Jewish rebellion beginning 167 BC, the loss of Jerusalem to the Maccabees in 164 BC, and his untimely death in the latter part of that same year, how could Antiochus be "exceedingly great" with a dismal military record like this?

4. Look at Daniel 8–9.

---

[5] https://web.archive.org/web/20170819194021/http://mcadams.posc.mu.edu/txt/ah/Livy/Livy45.html

> *[T]he great horn was broken, and instead of it there*
> *came up four conspicuous horns toward the four winds*
> *of heaven. Out of **one of them** came a little horn, which*
> *grew exceedingly great toward the south, toward the*
> *east, and toward the glorious land.*

Notice the phrase, "out of one of them." The pronoun "them" could refer to either the "horns" or the "winds." If it refers to the "horns," we could say Antiochus IV came out of one of the four Greek divisions. If it refers to the "winds," we would have to say this power came from the west because the action of the verse traverses from the west to the south, east, and southeasst to the *glorious land.* In Hebrew, words are masculine, feminine, or neutral, and a pronoun must either have the same gender or be neutral. In this case, "them" is masculine, "horns" are feminine, "wings" are neutral. This "little horn" —feminine—came out of the wind—neutral—and not the horn—masculine. Hence, the horn came out of the west wind, where the Greek empire had not reached. Antiochus IV was already part of Alexander's empire and the "four conspicuous horns." He did not come out of the west wind.

5. Antiochus IV reigned over the Seleucid Empire from 175 BC until he died in 164 BC. Yet, Jesus said, *"So when you see the abomination of desolation spoken of by the prophet Daniel, standing in the holy place (let the reader understand), then let those who are in Judea flee to the mountains"* (Matt. 24:15, 16). This event did not occur until AD 66, over 230 years after Antiochus IV's death,

and Jesus could in no way be referring to what he did in the temple.

For these reasons, Antiochus IV Epiphanes could not be the little horn of Daniel 7 and 8 or the king of the north in Daniel 11.

Rome Rises

> *But he who comes against him shall do according to his own will, and no one shall stand against him.* (Dan. 11:16)

After Antiochus III invaded Asia Minor, he was met by the Romans in 191 BC at the Battle of Thermopylae and was soundly defeated there.

In 188 BC, the Republic of Rome was clearly the dominant power in the Mediterranean region, implementing the Treaty of Apamea where Antiochus III of Seleucia lost almost all of his territory in Asia Minor. Moreover, the Romans refused to give territory back to the Ptolemies that Antiochus had conquered. Recall that a kingdom in Daniel 11 ends where the rising power checkmates the kingdom even though the previous kingdom may continue for many years because prophecy states *"their lives were prolonged for a season and a time."* In Daniel 11:19, Greece now moves off the scene and yields to rising Rome.

As discussed earlier, shortly after this time, Judea shed their Seleucids oppressors in the Maccabean Revolt of 163 BC and established a semi-independent nation until Pompey and the Romans besieged and seized Judea in 63 BC.

Daniel 11:3–19 Interpretation verse by verse

Daniel 11 is highly detailed on the Hellenistic Kings of the North and the South from 301–188 BC. Here we will look at interpretation verse by verse in the following section:

3 Then a mighty king shall arise, who shall rule with great dominion, and do according to his will.

> This is a major power transition from Persia to Greece with Alexander the Great (336–323 BC).

4. And when he has arisen, his kingdom shall be broken up and divided toward the four winds of heaven, but not among his posterity nor according to his dominion with which he ruled; for his kingdom shall be uprooted, even for others besides these.

> This refers to the Greek Diadochi with (1) Macedonia under Cassander; (2) Thrace and NW Asia Minor under Lysimachus; (3) Egypt under Ptolemy; and (4) Syria and Babylonia under Seleucus.

5. Also the king of the South shall become strong, as well as one of his princes; and he shall gain power over him and have dominion. His dominion shall be a great dominion.

The scene shifts from 4 divisions of Greece to Ptolemy in Egypt; The King of the South is Ptolemy I Soter (322–285 BC); The King of the North is Seleucus 1 Nicator (312–280 BC), who was one of the princes of Alexander and ruled from Syria to India.

6. *And at the end of some years they shall join forces, for the daughter of the king of the South shall go to the king of the North to make an agreement; but she shall not retain the power of her authority, and neither he nor his authority shall stand; but she shall be given up, with those who brought her, and with him who begot her, and with him who strengthened her in those times.*

The daughter of Ptolemy II was Berenice, who married the King of the North, Antiochus II Theos (261–246 BC). Berenice was eventually murdered by Antiochus II Theos's first wife, Laodice.

7. *But from a branch of her roots one shall arise in his place, who shall come with an army, enter the fortress of the king of the North, and deal with them and prevail.*

Berenice's brother, Ptolemy III Euergetes (246–221 BC), avenged Berenice's murder. The King of the North is Seleucus II Kallinikos (246–226 BC), who was son of Laodice.

8. *And he shall also carry their gods captive to Egypt, with their princes and their precious articles of silver and gold; and he shall continue more years than the king of the North.*

Ptolemy III Euergetes retrieved from Syria the images of the gods removed by Cambyses of Persia.

9. *Also the king of the North shall come to the kingdom of the king of the South, but shall return to his own land.*

Seleucus II Kallinikos made a brief foray towards Egypt but was repulsed and forced to return to Syria.

10. *However his sons shall stir up strife, and assemble a multitude of great forces; and one shall certainly come and overwhelm and pass through; then he shall return to his fortress and stir up strife.*

Sons of the King of the North were Seleucus III Ceranus (226–223 BC) and Antiochus III Magnus (223–187 BC). Magnus Marched against Ptolemy IV Philopater (221–203 BC, King of the South) but eventually returned home, conquering Antioch.

11. *And the king of the South shall be moved with rage, and go out and fight with him, with the king of the North, who shall muster a great multitude; but the multitude shall be given into the hand of his enemy.*

Antiochus III Magnus was defeated at Raphia on the Egyptian border in 217 BC by Ptolemy IV Philopater.

12. *When he has taken away the multitude, his heart will be lifted up; and he will cast down tens of thousands, but he will not prevail.*

Ptolemy IV Philopater conquered Judea, and upon return to Egypt, he zealously took on the traditional role of a pharaoh and lifted himself to heaven in the Raphia Decree, which contains the following line,

> There shall be celebrated a festival and a procession in all the temples throughout Egypt for king Ptolemy, the ever-living, the beloved of Isis, from the 10th of Pachon, the day whereon the king conquered his adversary, for five days each year, with wearing of wreaths and offering of burnt offerings and libations and all the other things which it is proper to do, and it shall be done according to the beautiful command.

Even so, a rebellion broke out in the Egyptian Delta and in Upper Egypt, where he slaughtered tens of thousands of his own citizens. Shortly after, in 203 BC, he came to an early death at age forty.

13. *For the king of the North will return and muster a multitude greater than the former, and shall certainly come at the end of some years with a great army and much equipment.*

Minor Power Transition KOS Ptolemy to KON Selucia: Antiochus III Magnus waged war against the Ptolemies and eventually took possession of Palestine at the Battle of Panium (198 BC).

14. *Now in those times many shall rise up against the king of the South. Also, violent men of your people shall exalt themselves in fulfillment of the vision, but they shall fall.*

Antiochus III Magnus and Philip V of Macedonia fought in an alliance against Ptolemy V Epiphanes (203–181 BC) of Egypt. Additionally, Rome was exerting pressure on Ptolemy. The "violent men" were Jews who opposed Ptolemy V.

15. *So the king of the North shall come and build a siege mound, and take a fortified city; and the forces of the South shall not withstand him. Even his choice troops shall have no strength to resist.*

Antiochus III Magnus defeated Scopas, general fighting for Egypt, near Caesarea Philippi, and then conquered Sidon, where Scopas had retreated. After this, Egypt never ruled Palestine ever again.

16. *But he who comes against him shall do according to his own will, and no one shall stand against him. He shall stand in the Glorious Land with destruction in his power.*

Antiochus III Magnus took over Palestine in 198 BC.

17. *He shall also set his face to enter with the strength of his whole kingdom, and upright ones with him; thus shall he do. And he shall give him the daughter of women to destroy it; but she shall not stand with him, or be for him.*

Antiochus III Magnus gave his daughter Cleopatra I to Ptolemy V, hoping to conquer Egypt through intrigue, but Cleopatra opposed her father's plans.

18. *After this he shall turn his face to the coastlands, and shall take many. But a ruler shall bring the reproach against them to an end; and with the reproach removed, he shall turn back on him.*

Major Power Transition from Greece to Rome: Antiochus III Magnus turned against Asia Minor but was turned back by the Roman general Lucius Cornelius Scipio in 190 BC. In 188 BC, Antiochus III was forced to sign the Treaty of Apamea. *Both* he and Ptolemy V lost all claims to lands Asia Minor.

19. *Then he shall turn his face toward the fortress of his own land; but he shall stumble and fall, and not be found.*

Antiochus III Magnus was assassinated while plundering a temple at Elymais (187 BC) to meet his tribute payment to Rome a year after his peace accords with Rome.

The Pride of Antiochus III, Magnus—The Great

Before we close this chapter on the Hellenistic Greeks, let us look at the pride of Antiochus III for just a moment. Recall earlier, Daniel 11 vv. 16–19 parallel vv. 36–39, with both instances describing the pride of kings. Yet, the first part of the book of Daniel, the Narratives section, also discusses the pride of a king, namely Belshazzar, the grandson of Nebuchadnezzar in Daniel 5. We read there:

> *King Belshazzar made a great feast for a thousand of his lords and drank wine in front of the thousand. Belshazzar, when he tasted the wine, commanded that the vessels of gold and of silver that Nebuchadnezzar his father[a] had taken out of the temple in Jerusalem be brought, that the king and his lords, his wives, and his concubines might drink from them. Then they brought in the golden vessels that had been taken out of the temple, the house of God in Jerusalem, and the king and his lords, his wives, and his concubines drank from them. They drank wine and praised the gods of gold and silver, bronze, iron, wood, and stone.* (Dan. 5:1–4)

A truly great and wise man, King Solomon, once said, *Pride goes before destruction, and a haughty spirit before a fall* (Prov. 16:18). Also, King David, who God said was "a man after my own heart" (Acts 10:22), plainly states, *"Love the Lord, all you his saints! The Lord preserves the faithful but abundantly repays the one who acts in pride"* (Ps. 31:23). Antiochus III died, as did Belshazzar, desecrating the things of a god he did not know.

4: Ancient Rome, Daniel 11:20–22

Armies shall be utterly swept away before him and broken, even the prince of the covenant.
—Daniel 11:22

4. Roman Empire (31BC - 476 AD)			
Daniel 2	Daniel 7	Daniel 8-9	Daniel 10-12
			Imperial Rome arises and destroys the Prince of the Covenant

IN DANIEL 2 and 7, we gather the overall characteristics of each kingdom. The description of the fourth beast is lengthy, but the interpretation is brief. We read in Daniel 7:17–18, *"These four great beasts are four kings who shall arise out of the earth. But the saints of the Most High shall receive the kingdom and possess the kingdom forever, forever and ever."* Here we see the angel is extremely short on the interpretation of four empires as if to say nonchalantly, "and they came to pass." The angel appears to have wanted Daniel's focus to be on the judgment and the eternal kingdom. Yet, Daniel is astounded by the fourth beast, obviously because his people, the Jews, will be going through this time, and he has to ask the angel specifically about this "terrifying," "dreadful," and "exceedingly strong" beast with "iron teeth."

Daniel's prophecy in chapter 8 gives another short description of the fourth beast. We read there in vv. 9–10a, *"Out of one of them came a little horn, which grew exceedingly great toward the south, toward the east, and toward the glorious land. It grew great."* This is essentially one verse describing the worst, most devastating, longest lasting beast power to this point from Daniel 2 and 7. In Daniel 8:9–10, the horizontal movement of the Little Horn is short, taking Asia Minor and Syria to the east, Egypt to the south, and Palestine. Then after conquering the known world, this Little Horn moves vertically to heaven. What are the crucial elements in the prophecy of Daniel 8? A ram, a goat, the sanctuary, and a boldface king, tearing down the sanctuary. It seems that the angel makes almost every other element of this prophecy of more importance than this horizontal horn.

Daniel 11:20–22 Interpretation verse by verse

With the background of Daniel 2, 7, and 8 in mind, we will go directly to the text in Daniel 11 and explain vv. 20–22.

20 Then shall arise in his place one who shall send an exactor of tribute for the glory of the kingdom. But within a few days he shall be broken, neither in anger nor in battle.

> For almost 100 years before Caesar Augustus came to power, the Roman Republic seemed to be in an endless upheaval. With new peace and prosperity reigning in

the new Roman Empire, all this changed. The victor of the Roman civil wars over rivals Pompey, Julius Caesar, and Mark Antony was Octavian, who took the name of Augustus Caesar. He did not immediately proclaim himself emperor but instead began taking on many titles, which gave him all the powers of an emperor without having to be officially granted the title, including:

- *Proconsular*—authority over the Western half of the empire and general of 70 percent of the Roman legions

- *Augustus*—religious authority

- *Princeps*—first-citizen or first-leader

- *Civic Crown of laurel and oak*—Worn on the head of Roman generals during the Roman Triumph parades

- *Consular Imperium*—the power of a tribune in the Senate to include convening the Senate and people at any time, putting forth business he wanted and being the first speaker, vetoing actions, and presiding over elections

- *Imperium Proconsulare Maius,* or imperium over all the proconsuls where he had the right to interfere in any province and override the decisions of any governor

- *Pontifex Maximus*—the high priest and administrator of the advisory or administrative of the pontifices, the most crucial position in Roman religion

Augustus instituted a tax and census system reform throughout the empire to make it more efficient. Tax farming had been the means for collecting taxes in the Roman Republic. The "farmer" pays the governor, or satrap, a fixed amount for the right to collect taxes in a specific region. In return, the farmer kept any profit but could take a loss if he did not collect enough taxes. Levi Matthew and Zacchaeus were part of this new Roman IRS, as noted in the last chapter. We read these words in Luke 2:1, *"In those days a decree went out from Caesar Augustus that all the world should be registered."* Here we have a direct link from Daniel 11 to Jesus.

Not only did Augustus institute an efficient system of taxation and census taking, but he also greatly expanded the network of Roman roads leading to the expression, "All roads lead to Rome." On these roads, the gospel spread to all parts of the world.

On August 19, AD 14, near Naples, Italy, Caesar Augustus died after some months of declining health neither in "anger nor in battle." Suetonius records the following in regards to Augustus' death:

> [H]e slipped away, as he was kissing Livia, with these words: "Live mindful of our marriage, Livia, and farewell." Thus did he have the good fortune to die easily and as he had always wished. For whenever he heard that anyone had died quickly and without suffering, he would pray that he himself

and his dear ones would have a similar "euthanasia."
–Suetonius, The Deified Augustus, 99.

21 *In his place shall arise a contemptible person to whom royal
majesty has not been given. He shall come in without warning and
obtain the kingdom by flatteries.*

While Emperor Augustus Caesar was in power at the
birth of Jesus, his adopted son, Tiberius Caesar, was in
power at the time of Jesus's crucifixion thirty-three years
later. Though a great military commander, he spurned
court life and politics. Augustus attempted to groom his
nephew, then a grandson, and still another adopted son
for the throne. Each died before Augustus, leaving only
Tiberius, the bottom of the barrel, left for the throne. In
AD 14, when Augustus died, and the Senate did indeed
proclaim him Emperor of Rome.

Suetonius Tranquillus, in his book *The Lives of the
Twelve Caesars*, states this about Augustus's will:

The will began thus: "Since my ill-fortune has
deprived me of my two sons, Caius and Lucius, let
Tiberius Caesar be heir to two-thirds of my estate."
These words countenanced the suspicion of those
who were of opinion, that Tiberius was appointed
successor more out of necessity than choice, since
Augustus could not refrain from prefacing his will
in that manner.

However, an uproar erupted upon Tiberius's entrance before the Senate to be bestowed the titles given to Augustus. Tiberius claimed he wanted no honors and just wanted to serve the state. He declined forcefully the titles Pater Patriae, Imperator, Princeps, the Civic Crown, and even that of Augustus.

Scott (1932), in his work, *Tiberius' Refusal of the Title "Augustus,"* states the following:

> Tiberius "did not assume the title 'Augustus'" (for he never permitted it to be voted him); still, when he heard it spoken and read it when written he suffered it; and whenever he sent letters to any kings he also included the title. (Wallace, 1939, p. 43)

> As we have seen, Tiberius' policy avowed in the senate was to remain for Romans a mortal, and consistency demanded, therefore, that he refuse to acknowledge the divine title officially in his dealings with them. (Wallace, 1939, p. 49)

Secular historians say Tiberius was initially a good ruler, but after the poisoning of his son in AD 23, he soon fell out of favor with the people. He became eccentric, aloof, and reclusive. He would leave the city to ruthless leaders who abused the people while he went off to the paradise island of Capri and committed numerous sexual debaucheries. Tiberius died a lonely, old man in AD 37.

22 Armies shall be utterly swept away before him and broken, even the prince of the covenant.

We can rephrase this sentence to make two complete and diverse statements:

- First, we have a political statement: "Armies shall be broken and utterly swept away before him (or the Roman army)."

- Then, we have a religious statement: "The prince of the covenant shall be broken and utterly swept away before him (or Rome)."

This text is unquestionably about the power of Rome through its crushing legions, not only devouring nations around them but, more importantly, being the power who through Pilate issued a death decree and carried it out on Jesus, the prince of the covenant. Even so, the Gospel of Salvation—through a condemned and executed innocent Man—spread like wildfire to all the nations of the world.

Only three Verses for Ancient Rome?

Ancient Rome only constitutes three verses: vv. 20, 21, and 22, in Daniel 11. How could this be the case of the most shocking and destructive of all the kingdoms Daniel has seen?

1) At Jesus's crucifixion, Satan was defeated, and a new power or kingdom began to rise. In Daniel 10:13, Michael has to fight the king of Persia conceivably to get the decrees for the exiles to return to Jerusalem to be written. We know Satan is the power behind the King of Persia resisting Michael. It would follow that any power, whether the King of the North or King of the South, who resists Michael, has Satan as their true ruler. So, we see the Jewish Sanhedrin allying with Roman Governor Pilate's secular government to place a death sentence on the prince of the covenant in 31AD. We have a church and state union with Satan as the power propping up the alliance. However, three days later, Jesus leaves the tomb and lives, defeating this church-state union. Now a new and different King of the North is ready to come on the scene. The horizontal horn of Daniel 8 has turned vertical and will become exceedingly powerful.

2) Both Paul and John state the "Lawless One" and "Antichrist" power was at work during their day.

> *For the mystery of lawlessness is **already at work**. Only he who now restrains it will do so until he is out of the way. 8 And then the lawless one will be revealed, whom the Lord Jesus will kill with the breath of his mouth and bring to nothing by the appearance of his coming. **The coming of the lawless one is by the activity of Satan with all power and false signs and wonders**, and with all wicked deception for those who are perishing,*

because they refused to love the truth and so be saved.
(2 Thess. 2:7–10)

and every spirit that does not confess Jesus is not from
*God. This is the spirit of the **antichrist, which you***
heard was coming and now is in the world already.
(1 John 4:3)

3) Finally, Rome ends where its parallel passage ends. Both
parallel texts end with death sentences, one on Jesus,
prince of the covenant, and the other on Jesus's people,
the *people of the covenant,* or those of us in these last days.

Armies shall be utterly swept away before him and
broken, even the prince of the covenant (or Jesus).
(Dan. 11:22)

And he shall pitch his palatial tents between the sea
and the glorious holy mountain (or Jesus's people).
Yet he shall come to his end, with none to help him.
(Dan. 11:45)

The *"glorious holy mountain"* is Jesus's people? Yes! We
also see this mountain in Daniel 2:35, where we read,
"But the stone that struck the image became a great mountain
and filled the whole earth." Furthermore, Psalm 48:1–2
states, *"Great is the Lord and greatly to be praised in the*
city of our God! His holy mountain, beautiful in elevation,
is the joy of all the earth, Mount Zion, in the far north, the
city of the great King."

For the reasons stated above, Imperial Rome begins in v. 20 and ends abruptly in v. 22 with the crucifixion of Jesus on Golgotha and the subsequent destruction of the temple in AD 70. Following this, the Medieval Divided Kingdoms period begins its rise to domination in v. 23.

The Historical Jesus

Let us turn from the Biblical text for a moment and look at what historians call the "historical Jesus." While a belief in Jesus as the sin-bearing Son of God always requires an element of faith, believing there was a man who walked the earth named Jesus, who claimed to be the long-awaited Messiah, needs only to look at the historical record.

The first century Jewish historian, Flavius Josephus, in his Antiquities of the Jews, Book 18, chapter 3, 3 gives this report:

> About this time there lived Jesus, a wise man, if indeed one ought to call him a man. For he was one who performed surprising deeds and was a teacher of such people as accept the truth gladly. He won over many Jews and many of the Greeks. He was the Christ. And when, upon the accusation of the principal men among us, Pilate had condemned him to a cross, those who had first come to love him did not cease. He appeared to them spending a third day restored to life, for the prophets of God had foretold these things and a thousand other marvels about him. And the tribe of the

Christians, so called after him, has still to this day not disappeared.

The Roman historian, Tacitus, in his account of the great fire in 64 AD in Rome, wrote in Annals, 15.44:

Nero fastened the guilt... on a class hated for their abominations, called Christians by the populace. Christus, from whom the name had its origin, suffered the extreme penalty during the reign of Tiberius at the hands of... Pontius Pilatus, and a most mischievous superstition, thus checked for the moment, again broke out not only in Judaea, the first source of the evil, but even in Rome.

Babylonian Talmud, Baraitha Bab. Sanhedrin 43a, probably written in the second century AD, has this to say about the "sorcerer" Yeshua the Nazarene:

And it was taught: On the eve of the Passover Yeshua [the Nazarene] was hanged. For forty days before the execution took place a herald went forth and cried, "He is going forth to be stoned because he has practiced sorcery and enticed Israel to apostasy. Anyone who can say anything in his favor, let him come and plead on his behalf." And since nothing was brought forward in his favor, he was hanged on the eve of Passover. (BT. Sanhedrin 43a.)

The reason behind this Jewish passage is to justify the trial and execution of a heretic that the Christians staunchly say was, in fact, legally unjust. The Jews readily admit to the existence of a man named Jesus who claimed to be a messiah, yet allowing the belief that they had treated him contrary to the law would give credence to the claims of the early Christians. They had to respond to this charge by the Christians. Recall the Sanhedrin's response to the guard's report at Jesus's tomb, and we see the lengths and desperate tactics they would use to cover up this momentous event:

> *[B]ehold, some of the guard went into the city and told the chief priests all that had taken place. And when they had assembled with the elders and taken counsel, they gave a sufficient sum of money to the soldiers and said, "Tell people, 'His disciples came by night and stole him away while we were asleep.' And if this comes to the governor's ears, we will satisfy him and keep you out of trouble." So they took the money and did as they were directed. And this story has been spread among the Jews to this day.* (Matt. 28:11–15)

These non-Christian sources confirm the historical Jesus, including that He (1) performed "surprising deeds," (2) was condemned to die at the time of the Passover by both the Jewish Sanhedrin and the Roman governor Pilate during the reign of Tiberius—a union of church and state, (3) was hung on a cross, the Roman method of execution, (4) appeared to His followers after the execution, and (5) continued to have a growing group of believers which spread even to Rome.

The End of the Jewish Nation

While in Daniel 11:22 Rome's power is checkmated, Daniel 9:26 brings out more on the phase, *"Armies shall be swept away."*

> *And the people of the prince* (or Rome) *who is to come shall destroy the city and the sanctuary. Its* (Jerusalem's) *end shall come with a flood, and to the end there shall be war. Desolations are decreed.* (Dan. 9:26)

The gospel records the curtain separating the two compartments of the temple being torn from top to bottom (Matt. 27:51; Mark 15:38), signifying no more sacrifices were needed to point to the true Lamb of God. The Romans could have destroyed the temple immediately, but judgment in the Bible is often delayed. While the purposes of God are not always known, it could have something to do with the demand at Jesus's crucifixion and *"And all the people answered, 'His blood be on us and on our children!'"* (Matt.27:25). Hence, the capture of the city and the destruction of their temple would not occur until AD 70 giving their children time to accept or reject Jesus for themselves.

The Jews again revolted from the Roman rule in 66 AD. Jesus gives us great prophetic insight into what occurred during this period:

> *But when you see Jerusalem surrounded by armies, then know that its desolation has come near. Then let those who are in Judea flee to the mountains, and let those who are inside the city depart, and let not those who are out in the country enter it, for these are days of vengeance, to fulfill*

all that is written. Alas for women who are pregnant and for those who are nursing infants in those days! For there will be great distress upon the earth and wrath against this people. They will fall by the edge of the sword and be led captive among all nations, and Jerusalem will be trampled underfoot by the Gentiles, until the times of the Gentiles are fulfilled. (Luke 21:20–24)

Ancient historians Eusebius and Josephus both attest to the Christians fleeing Jerusalem. In 66 AD, at the start of the revolt, the Jewish factions would not allow anyone to leave the city. Roman General Cestius Gallus surrounded the city, making any escape impossible. Cestius was unable to penetrate the city's walls, and his forces near the coast were likewise embattled. Not wanting to lose his supply line to the coast, he abruptly ended his siege and headed for the coast. The Jewish rebels then sallied out of the city, attacking Cestius's rearguard with viciousness. The Christians in the city, seeing the Romans had left and the rebellious factions were no longer preventing them from leaving, immediately departed for the city of Pella, almost a 1,000-mile journey to the foothills of modern-day Jordon. When the rebels returned, no one would leave the city alive again.

General Titus ravished Jerusalem, leveled the temple, crucified, slaughtered, and enslaved a significant segment of the population. Jesus foretold this occasion: *"So when you see the abomination of desolation spoken of by the prophet Daniel, standing in the holy place"* (Matt. 24:15). The Jews resettled the city again, and a final rebellion broke out in Judea over fifty years later. The Bar KoKhba revolt of AD 132–135 ended with Jerusalem razed to the ground, the scrolls of the Torah were burnt, the Hebrew calendar was prohibited, and all Judaic scholars executed. The Romans were so furious that Judean providence was renamed "Syria Palaestina." The remaining inhabitants not killed were hauled off and sold in "Hadrian's Market." On the site where the temple once stood, a temple to Jupiter was erected.

The Destruction of the Temple of Jerusalem by Francesco Hayez

Thus, we have the tragic and bitter end of God's Old Testament people, the Jews.

Jesus foresaw this and, just before His crucifixion, lamented bitterly over Zion:

> *Truly, I say to you, all these things will come upon this generation.*
> *"O Jerusalem, Jerusalem, the city that kills the prophets and stones those who are sent to it! How often would I have*

71

gathered your children together as a hen gathers her brood under her wings, and you were not willing! See, your house is left to you desolate. (Matt. 23:36, 37)

Oh, what might have been!

5: Medieval Divided Kingdoms in Verses 23–39

Forces from him shall appear and profane the temple and fortress, and shall take away the regular ~~burnt offering~~. And they shall set up the abomination that makes desolate. —Daniel 11:31

6. End-Time Divided Kingdoms (1798 - 2nd Coming)			
Daniel 2	Daniel 7	Daniel 8-9	Daniel 10-12
			Spiritual Rome attempts to destroy the People of the Covenant

A Note on the Christian Church and State Relations

THE ANCIENT NATIONS of Babylon, Persia, Greece, and Rome were polytheistic, with prolific pagan religious and cult practices seen everywhere. God's people were witnesses to these abominations and, at times, forced to participate or die. Even so, with the coming of Christianity in Europe, a new yet just as abhorrent practice arose. For the most part, the ancient nations combined pagan religion with state power, but this new repugnant practice combined Christianity with state power.

At issue in the Medieval Divided Kingdoms was that secular power was used to force one to convert or give up their sincere religious tenets. In this chapter, we will be looking at certain religious beliefs which many people feel are not supported by Scripture. Those who adhere to these beliefs have an absolute right to hold and follow the tenets of their faith. What is not acceptable is for those tenants to be forced on those holding differing beliefs. The Founders of the United States enshrined this in our Constitution:

> "Congress shall make no law respecting an establishment of religion, or prohibiting the free exercise thereof."

The greatness of America is that it provides freedom for all to worship according to the dictates of one's conscience. Nevertheless, as we will see in the Medieval Divided Kingdoms, church-state power ran amok over rights of individual conscience.

In 2000, Pope John Paul II confessed and asked forgiveness for the sins of Christian Rome during the Medieval period. In his Lent address for that year, the Pope stated:

> Let us ask pardon for the divisions which have occurred among Christians, for the violence some have used in the service of the truth and for the distrustful and hostile attitudes sometimes taken towards the followers of other religions.[6]

---

[6] https://www.vatican.va/content/john-paul-ii/en/homilies/2000/documents/hf_jp-ii_hom_20000312_pardon.html

We will be primarily discussing the church-state policies of Christian or Papal Rome in Europe. Yet, other religions and political power unions emerged during this same period in Germany with the Lutherans, England with the Anglicans, Switzerland with the Calvinists, and Scotland with the Presbyterians. The Byzantine empire had the Orthodox church-state union, and even Middle Eastern nations had Islam. The American colonies were not even immune to this evil either, as we see with the persecutions committed by the Puritans.

While everyone should have the right and freedom to worship according to their conscience, no religious beliefs should be forced on others, nor should anyone be compelled to worship against one's conscience. We have the examples of Shadrach, Meshach, and Abednego refusing to worship in bowing to the image in the prescribed manner in Daniel 3, which was in essence, a "law respecting an establishment of religion." And again, Daniel continues his worship routine even after it was outlawed, sending him to the lion's den in Daniel 6, and thereby "prohibiting the free exercise" of the religious tenets of his faith.

Divisions of Kingdoms and Churches

There are significant parallels between the breakup of the Greek kingdoms and the church-state systems of the divided kingdoms. To begin, Alexander had numerous generals and leading officials vying for his throne, but by 301 BC at the Battle of Ipsus, only four remained to divide the kingdom of Greece. At the Council of Constantinople in AD 381, only four

Bishoprics retained power[7] after the breakup of the Imperial Roman Empire.

Greece and Divided Kingdoms **Kings of Greece Divisions**	*Parallel Rulers* **Kings of Church- State Systems**
KON	KON Rome
Seleucusended 168 BC	ended AD 1798
KOS Ptolemyended 188 BC	KOS Constantinople ended AD 1453
Lysimachusended 281 BC	Alexandria ended AD 641
Cassander ended 294 BC	Antioch ended AD 637
Antigonus ended 301 BC	Jerusalem ended AD 637

In the Greek kingdom breakup, Ptolemy of Egypt came up first to control the Glorious Land in the south. Likewise, the Bishop of Constantinople, where the emperor resided, controlled the Christian church as "the seat of the New Rome." Some scholars believe Imperial Rome became the King of the North after the Seleucids were defeated at Thermopylae in 191 BC. If Christian Rome grew out of Imperial Rome as the King of the North, it would stand to reason that the King of the South would be a power creating a *"great conflict"* (Dan. 10:1) with Christian Rome. History describes a great struggle over the Christian church authority between the Bishop of Rome in the West and the Byzantine Emperor with the Bishop of Constantinople in the East. Moreover, Constantinople is southeast of Rome, and the Byzantine empire included regions south of Rome such

---

[7] https://en.wikipedia.org/wiki/First_Council_of_Constantinople#Shift_of_influence_from_Rome_to_Constantinople

as Egypt, west Africa, Sicily, and the southern section of the Italian peninsula. Hence, we see the King of the North in Rome and the King of the South in Constantinople.

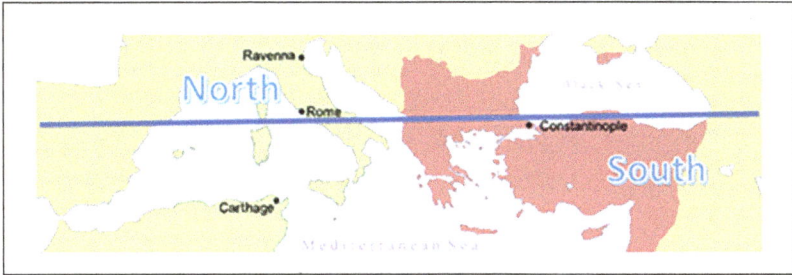

Byzantine Empire 527 AD

Previous Prophecies about the Medieval Divided Kingdoms

We will now consider the description and characteristics of the Medieval Divided Kingdoms in the previous prophecies of Daniel.

- Daniel 2—Divided church-state power in vv. 33b, 41–43

    its feet partly of iron and partly of clay.

    ...

    And as you saw the feet and toes, partly of potter's clay and partly of iron, it shall be a divided kingdom, but some of the firmness of iron shall be in it, just as you saw iron mixed with the soft clay. And as the toes of the feet were partly iron and partly clay, so the kingdom shall be partly strong and partly brittle. As you saw the iron mixed with soft clay, so they will mix with one another in marriage, but they will not hold together, just as iron does not mix with clay.

Note: *Iron* represents state power from the previous kingdoms, and the *clay* represents God's people or the church. In Jeremiah, we read: *"Behold, like the clay in the potter's hand, so are you in my hand, O house of Israel"* (Jer. 18:16).

- Daniel 7—Comes up among the ten horns in vv. 8, 20–21, 24–25

I considered the horns, and behold, there came up among them another horn, a little one, before which three of the first horns were plucked up by the roots. And behold, in this horn were eyes like the eyes of a man, and a mouth speaking great things.

...

and about the ten horns that were on its head, and the other horn that came up and before which three of them fell, the horn that had eyes and a mouth that spoke great things, and that seemed greater than its companions. As I looked, this horn made war with the saints and prevailed over them...

He shall speak words against the Most High, and shall wear out the saints of the Most High, and shall think to change the times and the law; and they shall be given into his hand for a time, times, and half a time.

Note: If Imperial Rome was located in Europe, these ten horns must come up in Europe also.

- Daniel 8—Attacks the Sanctuary Practices in vv. 10–14, 23–25

It grew great, even to the host of heaven. And some of the host and some of the stars it threw down to the ground and trampled on them. It became great, even as great as the Prince of the host. And the regular ~~burnt offering~~ [burnt offering is not in the original text, see explanation on page 11] *was taken away from him, and the place of his sanctuary was overthrown. And a host will be given over to it together with the regular* ~~burnt offering~~ *because of transgression, and it will throw truth to the ground, and it will act and prosper. Then I heard a holy one speaking, and another holy one said to the one who spoke, "For how long is the vision concerning the regular* ~~burnt offering~~, *the transgression that makes desolate, and the giving over of the sanctuary and host to be trampled underfoot? And he said to me, 'For 2,300 evenings and mornings. Then the sanctuary shall be restored to its rightful state."*

...

And at the latter end of their kingdom, when the transgressors have reached their limit, a king of bold face, one who understands riddles, shall arise. His power shall be great—but not by his own power; and he shall cause fearful destruction and shall succeed in what he does, and destroy mighty men and the people who are the saints. By his cunning he shall make deceit prosper under his hand, and in his own mind he shall become great. Without warning he shall destroy many. And he shall even rise up against the Prince of princes, and he shall be broken—but by no human hand.

- Daniel 9—Abomination of Desolation in v. 27c, *And on the wing of abominations shall come one who makes desolate, until the decreed end is poured out on the desolator.*

Note: Jesus spoke about the *"Abomination of Desolation"* being still in the future during His day in Matthew 24:15.

The Focus of Daniel 11:23–39

The above verses would indicate that Daniel 23–39 focuses on (1) the establishment of a church-state system, (2) in Western Europe, and (3) which makes decrees and laws replacing the covenant and the sanctuary ministry. Daniel 10–12 is also about God's people in great conflicts. While there are numerous significant events during this time period, we will only look at events directly linking the above elements that would presumably be included in vv. 23–39. The events build on one another into a crescendo just before 1798 to create one head of a church-state system in Europe who professes to be God on earth and has replaced all the "continual" sanctuary ministries, including changing the Ten Commandments. All this directly impacts God's covenant by keeping people who are detested, separated, and persecuted by the Christian church-state systems apart from the general society.

Greece's power rose while there were still Medo-Persian kings remaining, and Greece's kingdom continued as the Roman power grew. Likewise, the Medieval church-state kingdoms began rising while the Roman empire was in decline until Ancient Rome was finally overrun by the ten horn kingdoms of chapter 7. Now, if we look back at our parallel prophecy on Greece, we see one start date and two fall dates. Greece had one fixed start date of 331 BC when Alexander defeated the Persians at the Battle of Gaugamela but had a gradual decline starting in 188 BC with the Treaty of Apamea and ultimately ending the kingdom in 31 BC at the Battle of Actium.

Compare the Medieval Christian-state kingdom's gradual rise in AD 508 with the baptism of Clovis I, who went forth the conquering in the name of Christendom. Then in AD 533, Emperor Justin gave Pope John III an official letter authorizing him to have authority over the former Western Roma Empire[8]. Finally, in AD 538, the Ostrogoths were driven from Rome by General Belisarius, giving full force to that union. Papal Rome had full ecclesiastical control over the former region of the Western Roman Empire, including a temporal power to accomplish its dogmas. Now, we come to one fixed date for the end of Papal Rome when in 1798 the Revolutionary French Directory ordered General Berthier to invade Rome, capture, and exile Pope Pius VI. We see an apparent reversal of the process from

---

[8] https://biblehub.com/library/allies/the_formation_of_christendom_volume_vi/chapter_iv_justinian.htm

previous kingdoms having one fixed start date with a gradual fall between where the next power arises and the complete collapse of the kingdom. With Papal Rome, we see the opposite, with a gradual rise with a fixed fall date.

Kingdom	Start Date	End Date
Greece	**331 BC**	*188 BC* *Treaty of Apamea* *168 BC* *Battle of Pydna* *65 BC Greek* *Mithridates Rebellion* *31 BC* *Battle of Actium*
Papal Rome In the Divided Kingdoms	*AD 476 End of the* *Western Empire* **AD 508** **Clovis' Baptism** *AD 533 Emperor* *Justin's Letter to* *Pope John III* **AD 538 Ostrogoths** **defeated at Rome**	**1798**

Additionally, like the Roman Republic was a power on the rise and confronting both the Ptolemys and the Seleucids, Islam was a power on the rise confronting both Rome and Constantinople, eventually capturing the latter. Furthermore, Islam had engulfed the three Bishoprics east of Constantinople of Alexandria, Jerusalem, and Antioch by AD 641. While the Greek King of the North, Seleucia, was conquered by Imperial Rome, Papal Rome as the King of the North, on the other hand, will not be conquered by Islam because of the prophecy of Daniel 8:11 stating that Papal Rome will extend until the second coming.

While the capital of the Roman Empire was still in Rome, the Bishop of Rome was the head of all the Bishoprics, or church leaders in the various region. When Constantine moved the capital to Constantinople in AD 330, this changed dramatically. As the "New Rome," the secular protection and ecclesiastical authority migrated from Rome to Constantinople. This left Rome literally out on a limb of the empire. The popes immediately went to work regaining their position at the top of the universal Christian church. This led to tensions with the other Bishoprics and the emperor, who was the official head of the Christian church. With the Bishoprics of Antioch and Alexandria waning in power, the Bishopric of Constantinople worked hand in hand with the emperor.

On the other hand, Rome was surrounded by barbarian nations and almost certainly felt she must exert her authority in Christian ecclesiastical matters over the other Bishoprics. An example of this tension with the Bishoprics was seen in AD 445. Pope Leo disputed with Patriarch Dioscorus of Alexandria, insisting that the ecclesiastical practice of Alexandria be under his authority and control. His reasoning was based on Peter being the Bishop of Rome and was the highest authority in the church. Mark the Evangelist, Peter's subordinate, established the church in Alexandria. Therefore, the Bishop of Rome, or the Papacy, was superior to the Bishop of Alexandria and all other bishoprics.

The tensions between Rome and Constantinople resulted in the power struggle of the Great East-West Schism[9]. Issues involving the Iconoclast controversy—the veneration of images, the use of unleavened vs. leavened bread in the Mass, celibacy of the clergy, and the filioque. This last factor continues to be the main point of disagreement even until today. The First Council of Nicaea in AD 325 produced the Nicaean Creed or a statement of belief used in Christian worship. The issue was the West added the "and the son," or the filioque, where the Church in Rome wanted the creed to say "the Holy Spirit proceeds from the Father and the son." In contrast, the Eastern church opposed this and wanted the creed to simply say "the Holy Spirit proceeds from the Father" only.

One of the lowest points for Rome in the struggle of supremacy in the church was during the Three Chapters incident resulting after the Second Council of Constantinople in AD 553. Pope Vigilius refused to attend and issued a document forbidding the council. When he would not consent to its main edict, the condemnation of the so-called Three Chapters, the emperor held him captive in Constantinople for eight years.[10]

For many years, the schism amounted to a war of words and edicts, as is seen in AD 858, when Emperor Michael III deposed the Patriarch of Constantinople, and because Pope Nicholas I believed he alone had that right, deposed the

---

[9] https://en.wikipedia.org/wiki/East%E2%80%93West_Schism

[10] https://www.catholic.com/encyclopedia/pope-vigilius

Emperor and reinstated the former Patriarch[11]. Hence, the emperor deposed the pope.

The schism got bloody with the Massacre of the Latins in AD 1182. Catholics or "Latins" were murdered or forced to flee out of Constantinople. Later, in AD 1202 Pope Innocent III called for the Fourth Crusade. Still, things went awry, and the crusaders ended up sacking Constantinople in AD 1204, putting the emperor and the church clergy to flight and occupying the city for some years afterward.

Finally, in AD 1453 the Ottoman Empire captured Constantinople partly because the Byzantine Empire never fully recovered from the sack of the Latins. With the fall of Constantinople, Rome was the last Bishopric standing to retain open ecclesiastical authority and temporal power over Europe and the Catholic colonies around the world.

While Protestant nations began breaking away from the control of Rome in the Middle Ages, many set up church-state systems of their own which were just as oppressive in England, Switzerland, Germany, and other countries. Church-state systems still dominate many nations in Europe and around the world today, though most currently extend religious freedom to those who are not of the official church. Yet, we know and can see, ample signs that tolerance of individual conscience in religious matters could come to a swift end.

---

[11] https://en.wikipedia.org/wiki/Pope_Nicholas_I

Europe

*Political division in Europe, North Africa and Near
East after the end of the Western Roman Empire in 476 AD*

King Odoacer of Italy

While the exact Germanic decent of Flavius Odoacer is debated,
he was a barbarian soldier in the Roman Army who deposed
the child emperor Romulus Augustulus and became King of
Italy from AD 476–493. Odoacer, during his reign, was on
good relations with Pope Felix III; although he remained an
Arian Christian. This was a reason for contention with the
Byzantine Empire.

Three Up Rooted Horns (Dan. 7:8)

- The Heruli settled on the Danube River around AD 500 under King Rodulph. However, by AD 508, he lost his entire kingdom to the Lombards.

- The Vandals came down through Gaul and Spain and settled in North Africa, Sicily, and Corsica. Emperor Justinian wanted to reclaim the western portion of the empire and exterminate Arianism. In AD 534, General Belisarius defeated the remnants of the Vandal kingdom and expelled them from the Byzantine Empire.

- The Ostrogoths were also Arian and settled on the Italian Peninsula after defeating and killing Odoacer in AD 493. Theodoric the Great reigned from AD 454 to AD 526 and kept good relations with the Papacy. The period from AD 493 to AD 537 is known as the Ostrogothic Papacy, where the Arian Ostrogoths had in large part determined who would be Pope. In AD 535, after defeating the Vandals in Africa, Belisarius continued the war onto the Italian peninsula against the Ostrogoths in Justinian's effort to root out Arianism. In AD 537, Belisarius reached Rome and occupied it. It was soon besieged by an overwhelming number of Goths under their King Vitiges. After a series of battles, with both sides suffering from disease and famine, Belisarius defeated over half of the Gothic force at the infamous Milvian Bridge, sending the rest of the Goths to flight and ending the siege in AD 538. At this point, the Papacy was able to occupy Rome under Catholic rule, and the *time, times, and half a time* (360

+ 2(360) + ½ (360) = 1260 years) of the prophecy of Daniel 7:25 began.

However, in AD 552, the new Ostrogothic King Totila led a resistance against the Byzantines. Generals Narses soundly defeated the Ostrogoths, after which they lost their autonomy and their ethnic identity and merged with the Lombards. The Arian Ostrogoth's defeat at Rome in AD 538 began the 1260-year prophecy. *Ministry* magazine (1931) explains it this way:

> [I]t was the beginning of its downfall, and so opened the way for the development of the Papacy not possible as long as Italy, if not Rome itself, was governed by an Arian power, or indeed by any ruler whose authority was primarily civil.[12]

Seven Remaining Horns (Dan. 7:8)

- The Alemanni settled in the region of Switzerland. However, they were defeated in AD 496 by Clovis I at the Battle of Tolbiac and were absorbed into the Frankish kingdom and became Catholics.

- The Anglo-Saxons had settled in the region of Great Britain by AD 450. Pope Gregory I, in AD 595, sent Augustine to Britain, and he began converting the Anglo-Saxons. In AD 664, the Church of England at the Synod of Whitby declared its allegiance to the Pope. Augustine was the first Archbishop of Canterbury.

---

[12] https://www.ministrymagazine.org/archive/1931/08/why-the-year-538

- The Suevi had settled in the region of Portugal around AD 410. Arianism was soon introduced and continued until about AD 550 when they began practicing the Catholic-Orthodox faith.

- The Visigoths moved into the Roman Empire beginning in AD 376 after defeating the Romans at the Battle of Adrianople in AD 378. Under Alaric I, they invaded Italy and sacked Rome in AD 410. They settled in southern Gaul, but in AD 507, they were defeated by the Franks under Clovis I at the Battle of Vouillé. From there, they moved into the region of Spain. While the Visigoths became Arians in AD 587, the Visigoth King Reccared I converted and began a slow process of transitioning from Arianism to Catholicism.

- The Burgundians settled in the region of Southern France. Clotilde, a Burgundian princess and Catholic, married Clovis I, but war broke out in AD 500, and King Gundobad was forced to give the Franks an annual tribute. However, in AD 532, at the Battle of Autun, the Franks defeated and absorbed the Burgundian kingdom.

- The Bavarians settled in the region of Southern Germany on the Danube river. Catholicism to the populous grew slowly in Bavaria through its Catholic dukes. In AD 724, Pope Gregory II sent Bishop Corbinian to evangelize the region. Earlier, in AD 716, Bavaria became part of the Frankish Carolingians Dynasty and was then absorbed into the Holy Roman Empire.

- The Franks were Germanic tribes migrating from the Lower Rhine and the Ems Rivers into Northwest Gaul. Starting in AD 428, under King Childeric I and his son Clovis I, the Merovingian family dominated the other Frankish peoples.

Frankish Kingdom

Because of the magnitude of its presence in Church history, this kingdom needs more than a simple bullet point. Clovis I united the Frankish kingdom, was baptized into Catholicism, and ushered in Catholicism as the state religion over Arianism and pagan practices. However, the Franks were different from other kingdoms around them. Instead of just having a state religion, they exported Catholicism. They forced conversions of all the conquered peoples, often being the early military arm of the Papacy, beginning in AD 508 when Emperor Anastasius I Dicorus gave Clovis a Roman consulship. The following year, Clovis captured and executed a former ally, Ragnachar, king of Cambrai, and his brother, Ricchar, who would not accept Clovis's conversion from paganism to Catholicism and were actively recruiting defecting pagans to their side against Clovis. Even so, the later kings grew weak and did not expand "Christendom" much further. In the year AD 508, the prophetic time periods of the 1290 days/years and the 1335 days/years began from Daniel 12:11–12. These periods mark the abomination of desolation with the church-state persecuting power. This period began with King Clovis' crowning himself king of Franks in the Basilica of Saint Martin, Tours France, in the presence and with the blessing of Catholic Bishop Remigius[13]. In AD 1804, Napoleon at the Notre-Dame Cathedral in Paris, France, took the crown from Pope Pius VII and likewise crowned himself Emperor of the French.

In AD 732, the military leader and Prince of the Palace, Charles Martel, of the Carolingian family, defeated the Muslims in the Battle of Tours. However, he refused Pope Gregory III's offer to the title of Roman Consulship and defender of the Holy See, and he also declined the Pope's plea to come to his aid against the Lombards, a longtime ally of the Franks.

While Charles declined the Papal invites, one of his sons, Pepin the Short (or the Younger), conspired with Pope Zachary to depose the last Merovingian king and proclaimed himself king. Pepin not only expanded his temporal power but that of the churches also. At the bidding of Pope Stephan II, he defeated the Lombards, who were harassing Rome and the Church in Italy. After their defeat, Pepin gave the land to the pope known as The Donation of Pepin, which became the Papal States. The popes of Rome now not only had a wide influence over Europe, but they were also the legal head of their own nation-state.

Pepin's son, Charlemagne, expanded the Frankish empire even more, and in AD 800, the pope crowned him as Emperor of the Holy Roman Empire. From this point forward, the Papacy

---

[13] Mathisen. R. (2012). Clovis, Anastasius, and Political Status in 508 C.E.: The Frankish Aftermath of the Battle of Vouille, p 106. https://www.researchgate.net/publication/334291297_Clovis_Anastasius_and_Political_Status_in_508_CE_The_Frankish_Aftermath_of_the_Battle_of_Vouille

had ecclesiastical authority over all Western Europe, had a military arm in the Kingdom of the Franks and the Holy Roman Empire, and was now a sovereign state of their own, subject to no one.

Wildcard Kingdom

The Lombards, a Germanic tribe, descended from a small tribe called the Winnili, originally from southern Scandinavia, before migrating to the region of Austria and Slovakia north of the Danube river. The Italian peninsula had been ravished from the Gothic War between the Byzantines and the Ostrogoths. By AD 572, well after the fall of the Western Roman Empire, they had established the Lombard Kingdom in the north and central Italy. In AD 592, the Lombards were at the gates of Rome, Pope Gregory I negotiated with the Lombards and agreed to pay an annual tribute, and they withdrew. The Lombards would control the area around Rome, often harassing the city inhabitants and the church's clerics until AD 774 when Charlemagne conquered their kingdom at the pleading of the pope.

"Not Mix Together"

Daniel 2:43 specifically states, *"they will mix with one another in marriage, but they will not hold together,"* and this prophecy still stands today. Many scholars have researched the lines of marriages in Europe between kings and queens, as seen in this prophecy. Throughout the Bible and in the ancient world, inheritance was through primogeniture or the passing on of inheritance property and estate to the eldest son. But Europe was different. Whereas the Byzantine Empire commonly had one successor, many kings of Europe partitioned their estates between all their sons. Even if a king enlarged his region and spread Catholicism as the religion of the land, it would be redistributed between his heirs. This was the case with the Merovingian Frankish Dynasty of Clovis I and again with the Carolingian Frankish Dynasty of Charlemagne, weakening the kingdom after each succession. One attempt for European kings to retain power was to "*mix with one another in marriage.*" Still, of course, this was futile because the Bible prophesied against these schemes, and in turn, these marriage alliances often had devastating consequences.

Consequently, unlike Constantinople, where there was only one emperor to deal with, the popes had to continually maneuver and work with these kings and rulers. Rewards like coronations, titles, and relics, or by threats of anathemas, ex-communication, and populace uprisings were the means to retain power. Try as they may, they could not turn Europe into a unified and sustainable empire through bribery, wars, and intermarriages. This could not be done, and the prophecy of Daniel 2 still stands today despite the latest attempts through the European Union.

While Rome was located on the Italian peninsula, Catholicism had a difficult time rooting itself there. From the days following the transfer of the Roman capital to Constantinople, Rome was surrounded by diverse Germanic tribes such as Lombards, the Sicilians, Sardinians, and Ostrogoths. In the fifth century, while the northern section of the peninsula was under the control of the Ostrogoths, the lower portion was still part of the Byzantine Empire for many years and derived much of its doctrines and practices from Constantinople and not Rome. However, the Byzantine empire was out of the region completely by AD 751 when the Lombards invaded Rome, and the Pope had to seek assistance from the Franks. With the defeat of the Lombards, the Franks gave the region known as the Papal States to the Pope. In return, Pope Stephen anointed Pepin the Short of the Franks and titled him *Patricius Romanorum*. In AD 800, with Pope Leo III crowning Charlemagne Emperor of the Holy Roman Empire and giving him the title of *Imperator Romanorum*, the northern and central section of the Italian peninsula was solidly under Catholic temporal control.

Attacks on the Covenant and the Sanctuary

If a nation speaks through the laws it legislates, then it would stand that a church speaks through its doctrines and councils, and in the case of the Catholic Church, when the Pope speaks *ex cathedra*. It was evident from the progression of the councils, the churches of the East attempted to hold fast to the practices of the first century church by holding on to the Sabbath, forbidding idolatry, and allowing priests to marry. However, the Church in Rome was heavily influenced by the ancient Roman pagan practices and the pagan nations around them and slowly brought those into the Church.

One of the earliest pagan changes came between the second and fourth centuries, involving the day of worship. The Bible records no such change from the Sabbath to Sunday, and there is good reason to believe it was not changed in the apostle's day. If circumcision created such an uproar in the early church, imagine what the uproar would have been over changing the day of worship, but there is no change recorded in the Bible. The apostle Paul, during his trials, states emphatically, *"But this I confess to you, that according to the Way, which they call a sect, I worship the God of our fathers, believing everything laid down by the Law and written in the Prophets"* (Acts 24:14) and again, *"Paul argued in his defense, 'Neither against the law of the Jews, nor against the temple, nor against Caesar have I committed any offense'"*(Acts 25:8).

We also know from early church documents that the seventh-day Sabbath was still in practice in the second century. The Didache, or "Teaching of the Twelve Apostles," written around AD 65–80, while not explicitly mentioning the Sabbath, states, *"fast on the fourth day and the Preparation.[14]"* If they were keeping Sunday in AD 80, they would not allude to the preparation day. Also, the disputed Epistle of Barnabas, written between AD 70 and AD 132, uses "Sabbath" eight times with no references to Sunday or the Lord's Day. In the Epistle of Barnabas, in Acts 15:1–41, it states, *"Moreover concerning the Sabbath likewise it is written in the Ten Words, in which He spake to Moses face to face on Mount Sinai; And ye shall hallow the Sabbath of the Lord with pure hands and with a pure heart."* However, the writer states in Acts 15:9, *"Wherefore also we keep the eighth day for rejoicing, in the which also Jesus rose from the dead, and having been manifested ascended into the heavens."* So, we see believers still keeping

---

[14] http://www.earlychristianwritings.com/text/didache-lightfoot.html

the Sabbath and beginning their reverence for Sunday, yet not before AD 132.

While the change continued slowly in the second century, it culminated with the decree of Emperor Constantine in AD 321:

> On the venerable Day of the Sun let the magistrates and people residing in cities rest, and let all workshops be closed. In the country, however, persons engaged in agriculture may freely and lawfully continue their pursuits; because it often happens that another day is not so suitable for grain-sowing or for vine-planting; lest by neglecting the proper moment for such operations the bounty of heaven should be lost.

Past scholars on Daniel have correctly focused on the infallibility or *ex cathedra* statements of the pontiffs. Even so, much can be learned focusing on the Catholic ecumenical councils, and this section will focus on the actions of those councils which affect the true people of God. Much of this section is taken from the online article, "The 21 Ecumenical Councils."[15] All churches have counsels and statements of faith. Likewise, all people in all churches have the right to believe as they wish. The issue comes in when the government weaponizes a particular church's beliefs to enforce those beliefs on others. What we see in the following ecumenical counsels is the Church using state power to enforce their dogmas.

---

[15] https://www.catholic.com/magazine/print-edition/the-21-ecumenical-councils

We can glean much as to the mindset of Christian Rome through these councils, including:

- The usurpation of temporal power from the Byzantine Emperor in early councils from Constantinople to the pope controlling the Church from Rome with his own emperor after AD 800,

- The development and growth and Papal authority,

- The progression of persecution of heretics,

- The pagan influences including veneration of image worship acceptance,

- Tradition as being equal to, then superior to Scripture, and

- The development of the Mass and Eucharist.

Council of Nicaea, AD 325 Byzantine Empire

The first official empire-wide council at Nicaea in AD 325 was called by Constantine the Great. It was to determine the date for Easter, not based on the Passover, but on the first Sunday after the first full moon following the vernal equinox. While technically not linked to a pagan holiday, it did establish the foundation for the authority to "change times and laws." The council also established a creed that listed the beliefs of the church. While based on portions of Scripture, this creed and future adaptations would become of more importance than Scripture itself within the Catholic Church.

Note: While not forbidden, nowhere in the New Testament are we commanded to keep Easter holy, nor would it fall on Sunday every week.

Council of Laodicea,[16] AD 364 Byzantine Empire

This council focused on the Sabbath question. Both Sabbath and Sunday were addressed in canons 49 and 51, and the council's wording gives clear evidence that Western churches were all keeping Sunday, but the Eastern churches still regarded the seventh-day Sabbath. Additionally, it is interesting that canon 35 forbade idolatry, which is evidently why later councils do not use this term "idol" but instead would decree the "veneration" of icons and images was permissible. The idea is that one is not praying to an idol, but simply praying to what the image or icon represents, *i.e.,* the Saints, Mary, or Jesus.

Note: Jesus said in Mark 2:34 that He was *"Lord of the Sabbath."* Nowhere in Scripture is any other day commanded except the seventh-day Sabbath.

---

[16] Full list of canons from the Council or Synod of Laodicea: https://www.newadvent.org/fathers/3806.htm

Council of Constantinople I, AD 381 Byzantine Empire

Persecution of Arians began after this council. Arians believed Jesus was only human and not divine.

Note: The Bible teaches that Jesus is the divine Son of God, yet, criminalization by state or federal government for Arianism of such groups as the Jehovah's Witnesses today violates one's freedom of religion.

Council of Ephesus, AD 431 Byzantine Empire

While the veneration of Mary began before this time, the council codified an unbiblical belief about Mary which would give rise to prayers to Mary, vernation of her as sinless, the assumption or ascendancy of Mary to heaven, the immaculate conception, and finally, Mary being Co-Redemptrix with Christ. The Catholic Douay-Rhimes Bible of 1899 translates Genesis 3:15 as "*she* shall crush thy head, and thou shalt lie in wait for *her* heel."

Note: While the Bible does indicate Mary to be a righteous and upright woman, no texts suggest that she was anything more than the human mother of Jesus in need of a Savior herself like everyone else.

Council of Constantinople II, AD 553 Byzantine Empire

While doctrinally, little took place during this council, the significance is the display of animosity and struggle between Rome and Constantinople. This council actually led to the capture of the pope by the emperor, who released the pope only after he accepted the condemnation of the "Three Chapters." Clearly, in AD 553, the Byzantine Emperor in Constantinople had the upper hand, but the Papacy would not submit for long.

Note: Jesus prayed that we would be one like He and the Father are one (John 13). It is painful to see Christians fight with each other.

Council of Nicaea II, AD 787 Byzantine Empire

This council was over the continued struggle to bring idol worship, or "veneration" of images and icons into the church. The council condemned Iconoclasm—the attack on or rejection of the belief in the importance of icons and images. Further, the council upheld the adoration of icons and images that Protestants would rightly consider idolatry during the Reformation.

Note: The second commandment forbids the worship of idols (Exod. 20:4–6).

Council of Constantinople IV, AD 870 Byzantine Empire

Again, we have the issue of Papal authority over the other bishoprics and the emperor. The pope believed the emperor had to obtain his approval before appointing or deposing bishops. Following the pope's mandate, the council deposed Photius as the patriarch of Constantinople, officially ending a schism between East and West, at least for a time.

Note: Jesus said, *"render to Caesar the things that are Caesar's, and to God the things that are God's"* (Matt. 22:21).

Council of Lateran I, AD 1123 Holy Roman Empire

The controversy over church authority between the popes and emperors did not end when Rome created the Holy Roman Empire and subsequently divorced herself from the Byzantine empire. The emperor was appointing bishops in his kingdom, even though the popes said they alone should appoint bishops. This council eliminated the secular leaders from appointing minor officials in the church. Still, they could have an unofficial but significant influence on the appointment of bishops and important leaders.

Council of Lateran II, AD 1139 Holy Roman Empire

This council continued intensely to uphold nonbiblical practices in the Church by reaffirming infant baptism, the sacramental nature of the priesthood and marriage, the Eucharist, and condemning the marriage of priests. Catholic doctrine teaches that the priesthood merits grace out through the seven sacraments, including baptism. The more grace merited to a person by the Church on earth will ensure that person does not go to hell and will lessen their time in purgatory. The council also condemned all who did not believe the Eucharist was the physical, sacrificed body and blood of Jesus.

Note: In the Bible, a person is justified through repentance, accepting Jesus as one's Savior, and being baptized by immersion into the death and resurrection of Jesus to a new life (see Rom. 3:20–28). In the Eucharist, the bread and wine become the actual blood and flesh of Christ, and He is re-sacrificed every time the Mass is dispensed. The more Masses the lay member takes part in, the more grace is dispensed to them. Yet, the Bible is clear in Hebrews 7:27 that Jesus was sacrificed only once, which was sufficient for all.

Council of Lateran III, AD 1179 Holy Roman Empire

The council put the Papacy in a position to persecute "heretics" using the state powers in France and the Holy Roman Empire, specifically against the Waldenses and Albigenses but, in essence, anyone who opposed the official Church doctrines.

Note: Jesus never used violence, but only love and kindness.

Council of Lateran IV, AD 1215 Holy Roman Empire

This council revisited the doctrine of the Eucharist and defined "transubstantiation" to explain the real presence of Jesus in the Mass:

> His body and blood are truly contained in the sacrament of the altar under the forms of bread and wine, the bread and wine having been transubstantiated, by God's power, into his body and blood. Nobody can effect this sacrament except a priest who has been properly ordained according to the church's keys, which Jesus Christ himself gave to the apostles and their successors.[17]

Additionally, Penance was added as one of the seven sacraments.

Note: Jesus instituted the communion service at the Last Supper, saying, *"Do this in remembrance of me."* It is a simple service to keep Jesus substitutionary death in our minds. It was never intended to replace or add to His sacrifice.

Council of Lyons I, AD 1245 Holy Roman Empire

This council excommunicated and deposed Frederick II for heresy and crimes against the Church.

---

[17] https://www.papalencyclicals.net/Councils/ecum12–2.htm#Confession

Council of Lyons II, AD 1274 Holy Roman Empire

The difference between East and West was put aside to plan a crusade that never naturalized while tensions between Rome and Constantinople continued. This council did make a definition for the doctrine of purgatory:

> Because if they die truly repentant in charity before they have made satisfaction by worthy fruits of penance for (sins) committed and omitted, their souls are cleansed after death by purgatorical or purifying punishments... And to relieve punishments of this kind, the offerings of the living faithful are of advantage to these, namely, the sacrifices of Masses, prayers, alms, and other duties of piety, which have customarily been performed by the faithful for the other faithful according to the regulations of the Church.[18]

> Note: Purgatory is not found anywhere in the Bible. There are only two destinations, heaven or hades. *"And many of those who sleep in the dust of the earth shall awake, some to everlasting life* (heaven), *and some to shame and everlasting contempt* (hades)." (Dan. 12:3)

---

[18] https://forums.catholic.com/t/doctrine-of-purgatory-in-council-documents/214195/2

Council of Constance, AD 1414 Holy Roman Empire

This council specifically opposed the teachings of John Wycliffe and John Huss for teaching sola scriptura, denying the authority of the pope and bishops, denying the real presence of Christ in the Eucharist, and writing against penance and indulgence.

Note: Wycliff, AD 1330 to 1384, was seen as the Morning Star of the Reformation and translated the first English Bible. Huss from Bohemia, AD 1369 to 1415, is recorded as saying during his execution:

> God is my witness that the things charged against me I never preached. In the same truth of the Gospel which I have written, taught, and preached, drawing upon the sayings and positions of the holy doctors, I am ready to die today.[19]

The Council of Florence, AD 1443 Holy Roman Empire

Papal supremacy over ecumenical councils had been challenged from the earliest days of the Catholic Church. This council decreed:

> We likewise define that the holy Apostolic See, and the Roman Pontiff, hold the primacy throughout the entire world; and that the Roman Pontiff himself is

---

[19] Lechler, Gotthard Victor (1904). John Wycliffe and His English Precursors. Religious Tract Society. p. 381.

the successor of blessed Peter, the chief of the Apostles, and the true vicar of Christ, and that he is the head of the entire Church, and the father and teacher of all Christians; and that full power was given to him in blessed Peter by our Lord Jesus Christ, to feed, rule, and govern the universal Church[20].

Additionally, there was a last gesture to reconcile the Roman and Eastern Churches, but this was short-lived. Ultimately, the 1500-year-old Byzantine Empire/Roman Empire was going to fall to the Ottoman Empire in AD 1453.

Note: 2 Thessalonians 2:3–4 plainly states,

> *Let no one deceive you in any way. For that day will not come, unless the rebellion comes first, and the man of lawlessness is revealed, the son of destruction, who opposes and* **exalts himself against every so-called god or object of worship, so that he takes his seat in the temple of God, proclaiming himself to be God.**

Council of Lateran V, AD 1517 Holy Roman Empire

This was a significant council for Church doctrines on opposition to teachings about death, or what many call soul sleep, and it reaffirmed the doctrine of indulgences. The doctrines of the Catholic Church hang on the existence of an immortal soul. If a person sleeps until the judgment where people go to heaven

---

[20] https://archive.org/details/papalprimacyinth00shaw/page/51/mode/2up

or hell, the whole concept of purgatory is null and void. There is no need to buy indulgences or come to the Church for "graces" to help one's relatives escape purgatory. The Church could not let this teaching on soul sleep continue. It is thought if this council had reined in Church and Papal abuses, the Protestant Reformation may have been averted. Nevertheless, later this same year, Martin Luther would post his 95 Theses, protesting the ecclesiastical abuses.

Note: Jesus said at the death of Lazarus that he was sleeping, *"Our friend Lazarus has fallen asleep, but I go to awaken him"* (John 11:11). When Stephan was stoned to death, the Bible records that he fell asleep (Acts 7:60). Regarding Jesus's second coming, Paul states, *"Behold! I tell you a mystery. We shall not all sleep, but we shall all be changed* (1 Cor. 15:51). Scripture is clear that at death, we sleep until Jesus returns to resurrect us either to go to heaven or hades.

Council of Trent, AD 1563[21]

Trent is the "final nail in the coffin" council by doubling down and codifying all the previous non-biblical Church teachings and erroneous doctrines in one council. Moreover, it attempted to counter Martin Luther's main emphasis on justification by faith alone. In the Catholic system, justification is doled out, little by little, through the seven sacraments. A sinner must

---

[21] Full list of canons from Council of Trent: http://documentacatholicaomnia.eu/03d/1545–1545, Concilium Tridentinum, Canons And Decrees, EN.pdf

come to the Church where the priests dispense the merits of salvation.

Note: Luther's study of Scriptures led him to discover that we are justified by faith alone because of Jesus's sacrifice on our behalf without works. Luther said, "The doctrine of Justification is this, that we are pronounced righteous and are saved solely by faith in Christ without works."[22] This short, concise statement uproots 1,000 years of Catholic teaching and dogmas. No need for the seven sacraments to earn salvation. No need for priests to forgive sin or dole out grace piecemeal. No need to buy indulgences. No wonder Luther was intensely hated, despised, and marked for death by the Roman Church!

Interpretation of Verses 23–39

Years of 508-ca 1453: Establishment of Church-State System in Europe (vv. 23–27)

(We will also be giving a loose interpretation of the parallel texts, not to supplant the meaning, but to see similarities, contrasts, and comparative themes to ensure we are on the right course.)

23 And from the time that an alliance is made with him he shall act deceitfully, and he shall become strong with a small people.

---

[22] Campbell & Satelmajer. (2017). Here We Stand: Luther, the Reformation, and Seventh-day Adventism. Pacific Press: ID. p. 43.

YLT: *And after they join themselves unto him, he worketh deceit, and hath increased, and hath been strong by a few of the nation.*

- The word *"alliance"* (ESV), *"league"* (KJV), or *"join themselves"* (YLT) comes from the Hebrew word *châbar.* Strong's definitions include: "to join (literally or figuratively); specifically (by means of spells) to fascinate:—charm(-er), be compact, couple (together), have fellowship with, heap up, join (self, together), league." The definition does not indicate that this is a written, formal agreement or an official peace treaty.

- Starting at AD 476, after the fall of the Western Roman Empire, the Papacy had to make temporary alliances with its barbarian neighbors in order to survive. Nevertheless, the alliance with the Franks beginning in AD 508, with Clovis, would not only be stronger than all the rest, it would remain steadfast until the time appointed of 1798.

- While the previous alliances between Odoacer and the Ostrogoths were necessary for survival but short-lived, the most important alliance was between the Papacy and the Frankish kingdom. Unlike the Arian Theodoric of the Ostrogoths, Clovis I, after his baptism, declared Catholicism to be the state religion and subsequently forced all the people of the lands he conquered to convert. It is said at the Battle of Tolbiac in AD 496, Clovis and his Franks were losing the battle, but he prayed to the God of his Catholic wife, Clotilde, and promised to become a Christian. Regarding the conversion of pagan nations in Western Europe, J.A. Wylie (1888), "the Franks leading the way, and earning for themselves the title of the 'eldest son of the Church.'"[23]

- Importance of the Year 508:

The Papacy after AD 476 was surrounded by barbarian nations who were either pagan or Arian and often co-opted and manipulated Rome for their personal benefit. With Clovis conquering, enlarging his domain, and converting his subjects to Catholicism, the pope in Rome and the Emperor Anastasius in Constantinople took note that this powerful nation could rid the western empire of the Arian pagan barbarians, which had plagued them since AD 476.

  o Gregory of Tours theatrical account of what happened in 508:

    Clovis received an appointment to the consulship from the Emperor Anastasius, and in the church of the blessed Martin, he clad himself in the purple tunic and chlamys, and placed a diadem on his head. Then he mounted his horse, and in the most generous manner he gave gold and silver as he passed along the way which is between the gate of the entrance [of the church of St. Martin] and the church of the city, scattering it among the people who were there with his own hand, and from

---

[23] http://historicism.net/readingmaterials/thePapacy.pdf

that day he was called consul or Augustus. Leaving Tours he went to Paris and there he established the seat of his kingdom. There also Theodoric came to him. (History of the Franks Book II, no. 38)

Many historians question Gregory's account. However, what can be said for sure is Gregory, and by extension, the Catholic Church believed the account to be fact, including "the wearing of the diadem was the operative act of succession that placed the seal of approval upon being hailed as Augustus."[24]

o   Based on the Battle of Vouillé in AD 507, Dr. Frank W. Hardy suggests the following events connected with Clovis occurred in AD 508[25]:

(a) Emperor Anastasius I Dicorus (AD 491–518) gives Clovis an honorary consulship in celebration of his victory over Alaric,

(b) Clovis asserts his status as a conqueror by riding through the streets of Tours, showering bystanders with coins,

(c) he eliminates a number of rival Frankish kings,

[24] Mathisen. R. (2012). Clovis, Anastasius, and Political Status in 508 C.E.: The Frankish Aftermath of the Battle of Vouille, p 97. https://www.researchgate.net/publication/334291297_Clovis_Anastasius_and_Political_Status_in_508_CE_The_Frankish_Aftermath_of_the_Battle_of_Vouille

[25] http://www.historicism.org/Documents/Clovis_and_508.pdf

(d) he establishes his capital in Paris,

(e) he publishes a law code that had been in preparation earlier, and finally,

(f) on Christmas day, he accepts Catholic baptism at Tours from the aged and saintly Bishop Remigius.

- With Clovis conquering barbarian and Arian nations for the Church and after being bestowed the title of Imperial Roman Consul in the year AD 508, a 1290-year reign began with Catholicism as the official state religion of France until 1798. The Papacy was given a temporal power in AD 508 to enforce the emperor's letter of AD 533, which gave the Bishop of Rome all authority in the church, and finally, in AD 538, with the liberation of Rome from the last Arian nation, the popes had dominion free from paganism and Arianism.

- Christianity started small in Western Europe but took over the south-central portion of the cotenant by AD 600. However, even with an alliance with the Franks, the Papal dominion was still basically confined to the city of Rome or this "small people" where the Church was even under Ostrogothic control until General Belisarius cleared out the remaining Goths from the city in AD 538. The citizenry of Rome was still suffering from the barbarian sackings, war, and famine.

Christianity in 325D (Dark Blue) and 600AD (Light Blue)

Parallel text: 3 "Then a mighty king shall arise, who shall rule with great dominion and do as he wills."

The Papacy was, in fact, able to do precisely this, albeit through planning, plotting, and schemes.

24 *Without warning he shall come into the richest parts* [among the richest men] *of the province, and he shall do what neither his fathers nor his fathers' fathers have done, scattering among them plunder, spoil, and goods. He shall devise plans against strong-holds, but only for a time.*

- In AD 533, the Papacy began the process of receiving a temporal dominion.

- The process of gaining land and temporal authority was a major goal of the Papacy throughout the early medieval times. By AD 756, the pope had the dominion Daniel was told about in chapter 7.

  o Prior to 533, the Papacy's only semi-independent property was the Lateran Palace, which Constantine likely gave soon after he "converted" in AD 312.

  o The Duchy of Rome, although officially ruled under the Byzantine Exarchate of Ravenna, was presented to the Bishop of Rome in AD 533. With the expulsion of the Ostrogoths from Rome by General Belisarius in AD 538, the Papacy had a small dominion in Rome, and the 1260-year prophecy began.

  o In AD 728, the Donation of Sutri by the king of the Lombards formed the first extension of independent Papal territory located on the border of the Duchy of Rome. It contained the strategic fortified castle Sutri overlooking the road into Tuscany.

  o In AD 756, the Donation of Pepin of the Papal States gave the Papacy a large independent section of central Italy running from Rome to Ravenna. This was based on an alliance with the Pepin the Short (or the Young), who, in exchange for the Pope's blessing to dethrone the Merovingian Dynasty king, who was not spreading the faith for Christendom, would make himself king and starting the Carolingian's line of kings. Anointed by Pope Stephen II in AD 754, he then went to war against the Lombards, defeating them and giving their land as a donation to the Papacy. Pope Stephan may have used the forged Donation of Constantine in his appeal to Pepin to go against the Ostrogoths. Before the Lombards took the area, it was formerly the region controlled by the Byzantine Exarchate of Ravenna. Now the pope had a legal claim to an independent temporal kingdom of his own.

• *Simony,* the practice of buying and selling ecclesiastical privileges, church offices, or promotion, began as early as AD 498.

• Competing for the Papacy in AD 498, Symmachus and Laurentius both bribed Ostrogothic King Theodoric for his support to make them the pope using funds from the Roman aristocrats. Theodoric took both bribes, and then made Symmachus pope because he had more support than Laurentius. The final known act of the Roman Senate was a decree directed against simony, "shameless trafficking in sacred things was indulged in. Even sacred vessels were exposed for sale."[26]

---

[26] https://en.wikisource.org/wiki/Catholic_Encyclopedia_(1913)/Pope_John_II

- The pope of Rome had to "devise plans" to be a temporal ruler, using monastic establishments to spread spiritual rule throughout Europe and gaining leverage against the emperor who had the Bishop of Constantinople at his side.

- When Emperor Justinian I sent the famous letter to Pope John II, giving him all ecumenical authority in the church,[27] the struggle from then on was not of the primacy of church bishops. It was a struggle for the primacy of Rome over Constantinople. Technically, the Bishop of Constantinople was under the pope, yet, the former had the emperor's ear, and the emperor had the sword. This struggle of church-state power would continue until the pope had a stable, temporal militant army of his own.

- *"But only for a time"* is a significant phrase. The word *time* used here is the Hebrew word *'eth* and Strong's H6256 which basically means "the time of an event." Until the time of the end in 1798, the Papacy engaged in scattering plunder, spoil, and goods among those who honor them.

Parallel text: 4 And as soon as he has arisen, his kingdom shall be broken and divided toward the four winds of heaven, but not to his posterity, nor according to the authority with which he ruled, for his kingdom shall be plucked up and go to others besides these.

---

[27] http://moellerhaus.com/studies/JUS533.HTM

In AD 325, at the Council of Constantinople, Constantine divided his church up into the Bishoprics of Rome, Constantinople, Antioch, and Alexandria. Constantine represented temporal authority, but the Bishoprics had ecclesiastical authority. By AD 650, only two bishoprics remained—Rome with its northern power base in France and Constantinople with its southern power base around the eastern Mediterranean.

25 And he shall stir up his power and his heart against the king of the south with a great army. And the king of the south shall wage war with an exceedingly great and mighty army, but he shall not stand, for plots shall be devised against him.

- This describes the Gothic Wars of AD 535–554, ending all Arian opposition.

- While prophecy was fulfilled in AD 508, 533, and 538, the last of the three kingdoms to be uprooted continued to remain in northern Italy, and this verse ties up that loose end.

- The period between AD 493 and 537 is known as the Ostrogothic Papacy (KON). While the Ostrogoths were completely routed from Rome in AD 538, they were not totally defeated. By AD 546, they had regrouped under King Totila with 15,000 men and had briefly retaken Rome. In AD 551, Justinian sent General Narses (KOS) with a force of almost 30,000 men. In AD 552, at the Battle of Taginae, Northeast of Rome, Narses and his army defeated the Ostrogoths, killing King Totila, and went on to liberate Rome. Finally, at the Battle of Mons Lactarius, the new king, Theia, was killed. The army was vanquished. The remaining Ostrogothic populace fled back to the region of Austria and was either absorbed there or with the Lombards who would later occupy the peninsula.

- A note about "north" and "south:" The original "King of the North," King of Selucia was practically due east of Palestine, and Imperial Rome was more west than north. Egypt was not due south of Palestine but southwest. In our current text, the King of the South moves from the south up the Italian peninsula to attack the north.

- As to, *"plots shall be devised against him,"* this can be seen in the fact that the Papacy initially supported the Ostrogoths and then the subsequent interplay between the popes, Ostrogoths, and the emperor.

  o In AD 523, Pope John I's traveled to Constantinople on behalf of Ostrogoth King Theodoric see Emperor Justin I about his decree against Arian beliefs and plead for better treatment of the Ostrogoths. Upon John's return, Theodoric had him imprisoned at Ravenna for conspiring with the emperor, where he later died.

  o Between AD 530 and 532, the Papacy was occupied by Boniface II. He was, in fact, an Ostrogoth and elected because of the influence of Ostrogoth King Athalaric.

o In AD 536, Pope Agapetus I traveled to Constantinople on behalf of Ostrogoth King Theodahad to get the emperor to cancel Belisarius's preparation for the invasion of the Italian Peninsula. Justinian immediately refused. The pope dropped that matter altogether and moved to a Papal supremacy issue over the Bishop of Constantinople, which was doubtless the real reason for his taking the journey to the capital. The pope believed the Bishop to be a heretic, but Justinian supported the appointment. When Justinian threatened Agapetus with banishment, he is reported to have stated, "With eager longing have I come to gaze upon the Most Christian Emperor Justinian. In his place, I find a Diocletian, whose threats, however, terrify me not."[28] Agapetus appeared to be more lenient to the Arians by allowing them to convert to Catholicism but only as laymen and not to Bishops or priests.

o In AD 536, Pope Silverius approved Belisarius's entrance into Rome. Richards (1979) states, "What followed is as tangled web of treachery and double-dealing as can be found anywhere in the papal annals. Several different versions of the course of events following the elevation of Silverius exist."[29]

---

[28] Loughlin, James Francis (1907). "Pope St. Agapetus I." In Herbermann, Charles (ed.), Catholic Encyclopedia. 1. New York: Robert Appleton Company.

[29] Richards, Jeffrey (1979). The Popes and the Papacy in the Early Middle Ages, 476–752. London; Boston: Routledge and Kegan Paul. ASIN B01FIZI4RW.

Belisarius accused Silverius of being conspiring with the Ostrogoth and he was deposed in AD 537.

o   In AD 537, Pope Vigilius became pope with the support of Belisarius and Empress Theodora. Even so, this did not end well for Vigilius due to the "Three Chapters" Controversy.

o   In AD 556, Pope Pelagius I was selected to be pope by Justinian. He promptly reversed Pope Vigilius's condemnation of the Three Chapters.

Parallel Text: 5 *"Then the king of the south shall be strong, but one of his princes shall be stronger than he and shall rule, and his authority shall be a great authority."*

Theodoric was a captive in Constantinople (KOS). Still, he was commissioned by Emperor Zeno to capture and dethrone Odoacer, and in return, his people, the Ostrogoths (KON), could settle in the Italian Peninsula by 493.

26 Even those who eat his food shall break him. His army shall be swept away, and many shall fall down slain.

•   The Ostrogoths had given the Roman Papacy limited temporal power against Constantinople for a short time. The populace of the peninsula had been devastated by war, famine, and disease. Ravenna was, at this time, the Byzantine capital of the west. Also, the Papacy had lost control over Papal elections and entered the Byzantine

Papacy period, which would last until AD 742, with Pope Zachary being the last pope to seek approval from the Byzantine Emperor. The Papacy would not gain the upper hand on Constantinople until AD 800 with the crowning of Charlemagne.

Parallel text: 6 After some years they shall make an alliance, and the daughter of the king of the south shall come to the king of the north to make an agreement. But she shall not retain the strength of her arm, and he and his arm shall not endure, but she shall be given up, and her attendants, he who fathered her, and he who supported her in those times.

From AD 775 to 780, Irene was the Byzantine empress by marriage to Emperor Leo IV. When he died, she became coregent with her son Constantine VI to AD 797 when she blinded her son and had him dethroned. She was the sole ruler and the first empress to be the regnant of the Byzantine Empire from AD 797 to 802. The pope refused to recognize her because she was a woman. Theophanes the Confessor states that Irene endeavored to bring about a marriage alliance between herself and Charlemagne, the Holy Roman Empire emperor. The plan was upset by her trusted advisor, Aetius. In AD 802, the nobles in Constantinople dethroned and exiled her, placing Nikephoros as emperor.

27 And as for the two kings, their hearts shall be bent on doing evil. They shall speak lies at the same table, but to no avail, for the end is yet to be at the time appointed.

- AD 711 Pope Constantine traveled to Constantinople to end a dispute over the Quinisext Ecumenical Council controversy.

- Originally, Pope Sergius I rejected the Quinisext Ecumenical Council and was ordered to be arrested and brought to Constantinople by Justinian II. He was protected in Ravenna by its militia and died in AD 701. Neither of the next two popes ratified the council.

- Emperor Justinian II officially commanded that Pope Constantine appear in Constantinople regarding the Quinisext Ecumenical Council. While the pope went without delay, his real motive was the split over sacramental marriages. He ratified the council and returned to Rome in AD 711.

- In the negotiations, a compromise was reached where Pope Constantine gave ground on "Economia" or the council's handling, management, and disposition. Still, he held firm on most other Papal concerns. It was truly a compromise borne in diplomatic speak where many words were spoken but accomplished little towards ending the rift between the two parties. This would be the last visit of a pope to Constantinople and the Orthodox church until 1967.

Parallel text: 7 And from a branch from her roots one shall arise in his place. He shall come against the army and enter the fortress of the king of the north, and he shall deal with them and shall prevail.

Irene's legacy in the East was her anti-Iconoclasm atti-tude which she often had to hide from the emperor. However, image worship in the empire was advocated when she was regent. In the ninth century, we had Empress Theodora, whose life and regency nearly mir-rors Irene's and led the restoration of the veneration of images and icons, and ended the Byzantine Iconoclasm.

28 And he shall return to his land with great wealth, but his heart shall be set against the holy covenant. And he shall work his will and return to his own land.

- After AD 756 and the establishment of the Papal States, the territories of the Italian Peninsula gave direct tem-poral sovereign rule to the Pope.

- Pope Stephen II worked his will with the counterfeit Donation of Constantine, which was most undoubtedly in circulation during the period before the Donation of Pepin. Cairns, in his book, *Christianity Through the Centuries,* gives this description of the Donation of Constantine:

In the document Constantine greets Sylvester and the bishops of the church and went on to relate that he had been healed of leprosy and baptized by Sylvester. In return, he declared that the Church at Rome was to have precedence over all other churches and that its bishop was the supreme bishop in the church. He gave territories throughout his empire, the Lateran Palace, and the clothing and insignia of the imperial rank to

Sylvester. Constantine then withdrew to Constantinople so that he would not interfere with the imperial rights of the pope.[30]

- AD 787 Second Council of Nicaea—Approved idol worship and tradition over Scripture

- Thus, for the first time, we find an ecumenical council confirming that Christians must adhere not only to the faith of the Roman Church but also to its traditional practices. This is clearly set out in the anathemas,[31] or damnation, that follow from the council:

    o If anyone does not confess that Christ our God can be represented in His humanity, let him be anathema.

    o If anyone does not accept representation in the art of evangelical scenes, let him be anathema.

    o If anyone does not salute such representations as standing for the Lord and His saints, let him be anathema.

    o If anyone rejects any written or unwritten tradition of the Church, let him be anathema.

---

[30] Cairns, E. (1954). Christianity Through the Centuries: A History of the Christian Church. Zondervan: MI., p. 183.

[31] https://www.papalencyclicals.net/councils/ecum07.htm

- Pope Adrian I consolidated Papal power, had a wide-ranging domestic policy, and rebuilt Rome's infrastructure, including aqueducts and basilicas. He reigned for twenty-two years and died in AD 795

Parallel text: 8 He shall also carry off to Egypt their gods with their metal images and their precious vessels of silver and gold, and for some years he shall refrain from attacking the king of the north.

  o The Pope and western Catholicism began venerating images and icons early in Church history, but Eastern churches discouraged this practice.

  o The Eastern churches were champions of Iconoclasm with the objective to destroy icons and other images or monuments, which was a major issue with the Western Catholic Church.

  o With the emperor's support, the church in Constantinople outlawed icons in the east but left alone the Church in the west. In AD 754, Emperor Constantine V forbids the veneration of icons throughout the whole empire. In AD 787, with the Second Council of Nicaea, the veneration of icons and images was restored throughout the whole church.

29 At the time appointed he shall return and come into the south, but it shall not be this time as it was before.

- The pope as KON attacked Constantinople as KOS again, but this time as a temporal power and not through a barbarian tribe.

- The Exarchate of Ravenna, a Byzantine Empire land holding, was captured by Pepin. Pope Adrian I authorized Charlemagne to take away anything from Ravenna that he liked. He took an unknown quantity of Roman columns, mosaics, statues, and other portable items, which were taken north to enrich his capital of Aachen. Ravenna then gradually came under the direct authority of the Papacy, although the archbishops contested this at various times.

- With the crowning of Charlemagne by Pope Leo III, the Byzantines and Franks (Holy Romans) were in a cold war. Unlike the previous hot war in v. 25 where the King of the South, through Narses, came with an overwhelming army, this time Charlemagne as the King of the North, with sizable force, attacked the Byzantine peripheral states of Venice and the Dalmatian coast similar to the U.S. involvement in Southeast Asia against the Communists. The Byzantines were not in a position to send a large force to their aid.

- Cairns gives this report:

Considerable emphasis should be given to the influence of Charlemagne in medieval history. His coronation marked the reconciliation and union of the population of the old Roman Empire with the Teutonic conquer. It ended the dream of the Easter emperor to regain for the Eastern segment of the Roman Empire the areas lost to the barbarians in the West in the fifth century. Because the pope had crowned Charlemagne, his position was enhanced as one to whom rulers owed their crowns; and the emperor was bound to aid him when he was in difficulty. Charlemagne's coronation marked the peak of Frankish power that begun with Clovis decision to become a Christian.[32]

- In addition to Charlemagne's advances in the Byzantium west, the pope refused to acknowledge Irene as Byzantine Emperor in AD 797. The Byzantines were defending the empire to the east with the Arabs and could not devote much effort against the Franks.

- In AD 811, a peace treaty was finally signed between Charlemagne and Byzantine Emperor Michael I. The Byzantine Empire would accept Charlemagne as king of the Franks, and he gave back the Dalmatian coast region. On the other hand, the Venetians allied with the Franks possibly to free themselves from Byzantine control.

Parallel text: 9 Then the latter shall come into the realm of the king of the south but shall return to his own land.

---

[32] Cairns, E. (1954). Christianity Through the Centuries: A History of the Christian Church. Zondervan: Grand Rapids, MI. p. 188.

Charlemagne entered the territories of Byzantine of northeast Italy and the Balkan Peninsula but soon returned to his kingdom land.

30 For ships of Kittim shall come against him, and he shall be afraid and withdraw, and shall turn back and be enraged and take action against the holy covenant. He shall turn back and pay attention to those who forsake the holy covenant.

- Out of their Mediterranean Sea bases, Arab pirate raiders sacked Rome in AD 843, which caused the Papacy to form the Italian League of Papal, Neapolitan, Amalfitan, and Gaetan ships to fend off the Arab pirates and winning the famous naval Battle of Ostia in AD 849.

- There has been much debate over where Kittim is located. In fact, the Septuagint uses Rome here instead of Kittem. While it is known that the physical location is on the Island of Cyprus, no historical account fits this prophetic description during this time period. Some have seen Kittem as a description of all Mediterranean islands in general. The Jewish Encyclopedia states, "Nevertheless the term "isles of Kittim" (Jer. ii. 10; Ezek. xxvii. 6) indicates that "Kittim" signified all the islands and coastlands of the West, and, according to I Macc. i. 1 (ΧΧεττείμ) and viii. 5 (Καρραιτέων βασιλέα), included Macedonia, and, according to Dan. xi. 30, even Italy."[33]

---

[33] http://www.jewishencyclopedia.com/articles/4825-cyprus

- Initially protected by the Byzantine navy, Rome found itself in need of a naval force of its own following the Muslim raid on Rome in AD 843 and the sack of the basilicas of Old St Peter's and St Paul's-Outside-the-Walls in AD 846. The Italian league of Papal, Neapolitan, Amalfitan, and Gaetan ships fended off the Muslim pirates during the naval Battle of Ostia in AD 849.

The Battle of Ostia - by Raphael

- The covenant was attacked with the sanctioning of idolatry and veneration of Mary.

- In AD 870, the Fourth Council of Constantinople declared:

  We decree that the sacred image of our Lord Jesus Christ, the liberator and Savior of all people, must be venerated with the same honor as is given the book of the holy Gospels. For as through the language of the words contained in this book all can reach salvation, so, due to the action which these images exercise by their colors, all wise and simple alike, can derive profit from them. For what speech conveys in words, pictures announce and bring out in colors[34].

If anyone does not venerate the image of Christ our Lord, let him be deprived of seeing him in glory at his second coming. The image of his all-pure Mother and the images of the holy angels as well as the images of all the saints are equally the object of our homage and veneration[35].

- However, early in church history, Mary worship was condemned by many. Near the end of the fourth century, Epiphanius of Salamis made the following declaration:

> For I have heard in turn that others who are out of their minds on this subject of this holy Ever-virgin, have done their best and are doing their best, in the grip both of madness and of folly, to substitute her for God. For they say that certain Thracian women there in Arabia have introduced this nonsense, and that they bake a loaf in the name of the

---

[34] Gesa Elsbeth Thiessen, 2005. Theological Aesthetics ISBN 0–8028–2888–4 page 65

[35] Steven Bigham, 1995. Image of God the Father in Orthodox Theology and Iconography, page 41.

Ever-virgin, gather together, and attempt an excess and undertake a forbidden, blasphemous act in the holy Virgin's name, and offer sacrifice in her name with women officiants.

This is entirely impious, unlawful, and different from the Holy Spirit's message, and is thus pure devil's work...

And nowhere was a woman a priest. But I shall go to the New Testament. If it were ordained by God that women should be priests or have any canonical function in the Church, Mary herself, if anyone, should have functioned as a priest in the New Testament. She was counted worthy to bear the king of all in her own womb, the heavenly God, the Son of God. Her womb became a temple, and by God's kindness and an awesome mystery, was prepared to be a dwelling place of the Lord's human nature. But it was not God's pleasure that she be a priest[36].

Parallel text: 10 His sons shall wage war and assemble a multitude of great forces, which shall keep coming and overflow and pass through, and again shall carry the war as far as his fortress.

With the victory over iconoclasm, the popes dominated the ecclesiastical authority in the Church from this point on. Only one more church council was held

---

[36] https://www.catholic.com/magazine/online-edition/the-assumption-of-mary-in-history

in the East, but even here, the Byzantine emperor was forced to consider the Pope "first among equals."

Parallel text: 11 Then the king of the south, moved with rage, shall come out and fight against the king of the north. And he shall raise a great multitude, but it shall be given into his hand.

During the Photian Schism of AD 863–867, the church in Constantinople challenged the authority of the Pope. The issue centered on the right of the Byzantine Emperor to depose and then appoint a patriarch without approval from the Papacy. Emperor Michael III deposed the Bishop of Constantinople and replaced him with another. The Council of Constantinople of AD 861 approved the actions of the emperor but was rejected by the pope. In the end, Pope Nicholas died, the emperor was assassinated, and the Fourth Council of Constantinople was convened to end the schism.

31 Forces from him shall appear and profane the temple and fortress, and shall take away the regular ~~burnt offering~~. And they shall set up the abomination that makes desolate.

YTL 31 And strong ones out of him stand up, and have polluted the sanctuary, the stronghold, and have turned aside the continual [~~sacrifice~~], and appointed the desolating abomination.

By sending the secular powers to enforce the dogmas of the church, the abomination of desolation was set up.

- The pope's "forces" were the temporal powers in Europe, the increased focus of the Inquisition beginning in the 1250s[37], and later with the Jesuit Order beginning in 1540[38]. These forces began to attack God's people after the Third Council of Lateran in AD 1179 with the condemnation of Waldensianism and Albigensianism.

- The Waldensians' beliefs included the atoning death and justifying righteousness of Christ, the Godhead, the fall of man, the incarnation of the Son, denied the existence of purgatory, voluntary poverty, opposed the authority of the state and the Church, and opposed the sacrament of matrimony. The Aelbigensians believed the Catholic priesthood was not needed, and they rejected the idea that the real presence of Christ was in the Eucharist and denied the existence of purgatory.

- As noted earlier, the translators supplied the words "burnt offering," which are not in the Hebrew text.

- Through the Eucharist and the sacraments, the daily/continual offering was taken away.

- At the Fourth Council of Lateran in AD 1215, it was ordered that parishioners must keep the annual reception of penance and the Eucharist. They also used the term "transubstantiation" to explain the Real Presence of Christ in the Eucharist.

---

[37] https://www.history.com/topics/religion/inquisition

[38] https://www.history.com/this-day-in-history/jesuit-order-established

- There is a completely different meaning between the Protestant communion service and the Catholic Eucharist Mass. Malachi Martin, in his massive work, *The Keys to This Blood*, explains:

> When you talk of the Eucharist, you are talking about the Roman Mass, which has been and still is the central act of worship for Roman Catholics. The value of the Mass for Catholics is twofold. In the Catholic belief, the Mass represents the real live Sacrifice of the body and blood, and the physical life of Jesus consummated on Calvary. It is not a commemoration of that sacrifice, nor a reenactment after the fashion of a historical drama, nor a symbolic performance.

> Therein lies the mystery of the Mass. When a Roman Mass is said to be valid, it is believed to achieve that mysterious presentation of Christ's sacrifice of his bodily life. It has validity, and Roman Catholics can then literally adore their Savior under the physical appearance of bread and wine.[39]

- In the Old Testament, the regular priests ministered in the courtyard and the holy place doing the "continual/daily" duties. While the high priest supervised the workings in the courtyard and the holy place of the sanctuary; only he could enter the most holy place and

---

[39] Maritn, M. (1990). The Keys to this Blood: Pope John Paul II versus Russia and the West for the Control of the New World Order. Touchstone: NY. p. 667.

only one day per year. God's New Testament people are a holy and royal priesthood of believers (1 Peter 2:5, 9). Martin Luther also believed this to be the case and that priesthood of believers flowed through Jesus, where Christians are to perform the basic duties of the Levitical priesthood.[40]

- In an article from an *Amazing Facts Inside* report titled *Secrets Of The Sanctuary*, the plan of salvation through the sanctuary is visualized in concise yet vivid detail.

  The sanctuary consisted of three principal areas: the courtyard, the holy place, and the most holy place. These three locations represent the three primary steps in the process of salvation known as justification, sanctification, and glorification, and they correspond with three phases of Christ's ministry: the substitutionary sacrifice, the priestly mediation, and the final judgment.[41]

- Symbolically, in the courtyard we are *justified* and have:

  o   accepted Jesus who was sacrificed once for all, and
  o   been baptized into his death and resurrection.

- We are now able to enter the Holy Place of the Sanctuary to spiritually perform the "continual/daily" duties of a priest:

---

[40] Campbell & Satelmajer. (2017). Here We Stand: Luther, the Reformation, and Seventh-day Adventism. Pacific Press: ID. p. 36,37.

[41] https://www.amazingfacts.org/news-and-features/inside-report/magazine/id/10734/t/secrets-of-the-sanctuary

o   before the Altar of Incense with our personal and corporate prayers,

o   before the Table of Showbread through Bible study and devotions, and

o   in front of the Lampstand, letting our light shine through our Fruit of the Spirit and our Gift(s) of the Spirit.

- Finally, we are ministers at the curtain separating the Holy from the Most Holy place,

o   symbolically sprinkling the blood of Jesus trusting in His merits as our Sacrifice and High Priest to provide us mercy and give us the strength to keep His commandments. Thus, we emulate His character of love in our lives and are being prepared for glorification at His soon coming.

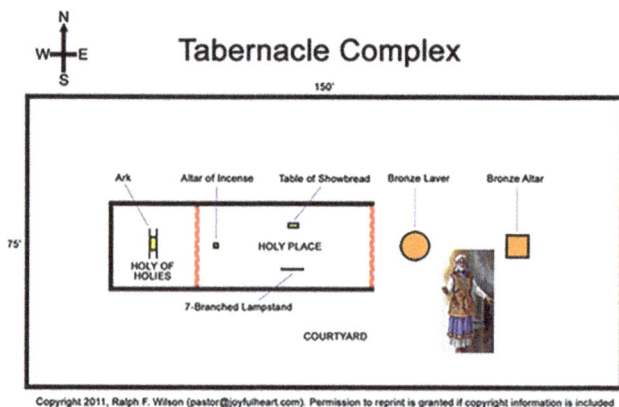

N
W—E
S

Tabernacle Complex

150'

Ark   Altar of Incense   Table of Showbread   Bronze Laver   Bronze Altar

75'

HOLY OF HOLIES

HOLY PLACE

7-Branched Lampstand

COURTYARD

Jewish Tabernacle/Temple

However, the Catholic Church has replaced our priestly continual/daily duties in the Sanctuary with the Eucharist and the seven sacraments.

- In the Courtyard:

  o Jesus is continually sacrificed in the Mass, and attendance is a sacrament to help earn salvation.

  o Baptism is by sprinkling, and it is also a sacrament.

- In the Holy Place of the Sanctuary:

  o Tradition replaced Scripture, and only the Church can interpret the Bible.

  o Praying the Rosary, and prayers to Mary and the saints.

  o Only priests can teach and bring others into the church.

- In the Most Holy Place:

  o Mercy is dispensed by the Church, and specifically, through Mary, the Mother of Mercy.[42]

---

[42] https://www.thedivinemercy.org/articles/
why-do-we-call-mary-mother-mercy

o The Ten Commandments were changed. The Catholic Church removed the second commandment, allowing for idolatry, then shortening the fourth to just "Remember to keep holy the Sabbath day" and transferring the solemnity of the Sabbath to Sunday, finally making the tenth commandment into two commandments to maintain "Ten" Commandments.

God's people are priests in the holy place of the sanctuary. Still, only their priests can enter the holy place in the Catholic Church, and they dispense salvation piecemeal through the seven sacraments to the parishioners.

Parallel text: 12 And when the multitude is taken away, his heart shall be exalted, and he shall cast down tens of thousands, but he shall not prevail.

In AD 1453, Constantinople fell to the Ottoman Empire, and the multitude of opponents to Papal supremacy ended. In AD 1563, the Council of Trent cemented all the errors of the Church, and the Church persecuted anyone who would not follow Church dogmas. Catholicism would not prevail because, within 250 years, their church-state system will be replaced with an atheistic-state system in France and a Protestant separation of church and the state system in America.

Years of ca 1209—1798: Protestant Reformation
Verses 32–35

(We will not give a complete interpretation of the parallel texts, yet they are listed so we can see similarities, contrasts, and comparative themes.)

32 He shall seduce with flattery those who violate the covenant, but the people who know their God shall stand firm and take action

Parallel text: 13 For the king of the north shall again raise a multitude, greater than the first. And after some years he shall come on with a great army and abundant supplies.

- Suggested Interpretation: Those who violate the covenant are those who choose to accept tradition and Church dogma over Scripture.

- Malachi Martin reflects on the medieval Papacy stating, "During the first thousand years of Christianity papal Rome [was] as a visible power among men—from 400 to 1400 ASD—the Roman papacy and its ecclesiastical structure, the Church, were the fashioners of the Western culture and tradition."[43]

- This "flattery" or smooth things can be seen in the praise for Pope Pius V who standardized the Mass in the

---

[43] Maritn, M. (1990). The Keys to this Blood: Pope John Paul II versus Russia and the West for the Control of the New World Order. Touchstone: NY. p. 501.

Roman Missal, which was produced in AD 1570 after the entreaty of the Council of Trent of AD 1563. Pope Pius issued the *Quo primum* (from the first) Papal Bull making his missal mandatory throughout the Catholic Church and remained unchanged for 400 years.

- The Catholic Church worked hand in hand with the Habsburg Dynasty against the Protestant Reformation overtly in Spain and Italy and covertly used the Jesuits in Central Europe. According to the "World of the Habsburg" website:

  > [T]he goal of making the mass of the population return to the Catholic Church was achieved not only by intensified pastoral care and pious works, but also through terror and violence. Habsburg state power rigorously destroyed Protestant ecclesiastical structures and persecuted non-Catholics mercilessly.[44]

- Shortly after the Third Council of Lateran, in AD 1209, the French military, under the orders of Pope Innocent III, began the Albigensian or Cather Crusade, which lasted for twenty years. Many were ordered to wear yellow crosses on their outer clothes, imprisoned, lost property, and were burned. On March 16, 1244, a massacre of over 200 was burned in a massive pyre.

---

[44] https://www.habsburger.net/en/chapter/struggle-peoples-souls-habsburgs-and-counter-reformation

- There are too many of God's true people who rightly fit the description of "shall stand firm and take action." While not the first nor the last, Martin Luther aptly fits this description. Dr. George Knight says by nailing his 95 Theses to the church door at Wittenberg, Luther's propositions:

> ...soon jumped the fence of separating the academic world from that of personal Christian piety and politics, and they ignited a revolution—a Reformation. Luther risked almost certain death for his challenge to the medieval establishment. But he was a man under conviction and moved forward despite the religious and civil powers arrayed against him.[45]

33 And the wise among the people shall make many understand, though for some days they shall stumble by sword and flame, by captivity and plunder.

Parallel text: 14 In those times many shall rise against the king of the south, and the violent among your own people shall lift themselves up in order to fulfill the vision, but they shall fail.

- In AD 1553, Queen Mary I, or "Bloody Mary," to the English throne attempted to mend the relationship between the English church and Rome. She repealed all religious legislation passed under Edward VI, and many Protestants were exiled, imprisoned, burned at the stake,

---

[45] Campbell & Satelmajer. (2017). Here We Stand: Luther, the Reformation, and Seventh-day Adventism. Pacific Press: ID. p. 9.

tortured, or punished in other ways. The Wikipedia article states, "Foxe's Book of Martyrs offers an account of the executions, which extended well beyond the anticipated targets—high-level clergy. Tradesmen were also burned and married men and women, sometimes in unison, "youths," and at least one couple was burned alive with their daughter. The figure of 300 victims of the Marian Persecutions was given by Foxe and later by Thomas Brice in his poem, "The Register."[46]

34 When they stumble, they shall receive a little help. And many shall join themselves to them with flattery,

Parallel text: 15 Then the king of the north shall come and throw up siegeworks and take a well-fortified city. And the forces of the south shall not stand, or even his best troops, for there shall be no strength to stand.

- Many Catholic sympathizers in Protestant areas joined with the Protestants to avoid conflict.

- With the full authority of the Pope and the Council of Trent, the Church persecuted and burned millions at the stake who would not succumb to their edits and dictates.

---

[46] https://en.wikipedia.org/wiki/List_of_Protestant_martyrs_of_the_English_Reformation

- In AD 1570, Pope Pius V codified all the previous developments in a new Eucharist missal which became the standard for the Western Church.

- Malachi Martin describes this mystery of the Eucharist in great detail:

  In the Roman Church, this mystery was celebrated in the Roman Mass, a liturgical ceremony that attained its traditional form in the early Middle Ages, was confirmed as a perpetual law in 1570 by Pope Pius V, and was recognized at the Council of Trent in the same century.[47]

- The Council of Trent in AD 1563 upheld tradition, stated salvation was not by "faith alone," decreed the Mass as a real sacrifice, defended purgatory, indulgences, the jurisdiction of the pope, and initiated the Counter-Reformation;

35 and some of the wise shall stumble, so that they may be refined, purified, and made white, until the time of the end, for it still awaits the appointed time.

---

[47] Maritn, M. (1990). The Keys to this Blood: Pope John Paul II versus Russia and the West for the Control of the New World Order. Touchstone: NY. p. 667.

- Ranson (2012) sees recantation as a normal strategy used by reformers to avoid death.[48] Copernicus, while his scientific discoveries were in a direct contradiction that Rome was the center of the solar system, quietly bowed to Church dogma. However, a contemporary of Copernicus, Galileo faced the Inquisitorial commission by Pope Paul V. His forced recantation read:

> I, Galileo, son of the late Vincenzo Galilei, Florentine, aged seventy years, arraigned personally before this tribunal, and kneeling before you, Most Eminent and Reverend Lord Cardinals, Inquisitors-General against heretical depravity throughout the entire Christian commonwealth, having before my eyes and touching with my hands, the Holy Gospels, swear that I have always believed, do believe, and by God's help will in the future believe, all that is held, preached, and taught by the Holy Catholic and Apostolic Church. [49]

- "[U]ntil the time of the end, for it still awaits the appointed time" is another specific reference to the time of the end in 1798. When did the persecution of the Dark Ages end? In 1798 when the Papacy lost its temporal power.

---

[48] https://historyandcultures.files.wordpress.com/2012/09/jhac-11-angela-ranson-sincere-lies-and-creative-truth-recantation-strategies-during-the-english-reformation.pdf

[49] https://famous-trials.com/galileotrial/1020-recantation

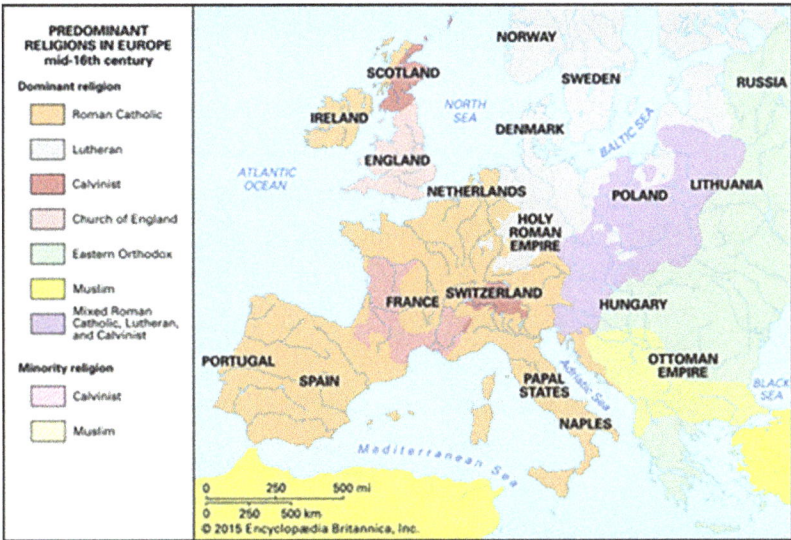

Predominant Religions in The Mid-16th Century

Years of 1453—1798: Full Power and Authority of the Papacy
Verses 36–39

36 And the king shall do as he wills. He shall exalt himself and magnify himself above every god, and shall speak astonishing things against the God of gods. He shall prosper till the indignation is accomplished; for what is decreed shall be done.

Parallel text: 16 But he who comes against him shall do as he wills, and none shall stand before him. And he shall stand in the glorious land, with destruction in his hand.

- At this point, the Papacy has reached the height of its power. The pope in Rome now heads the only Christian church-state system with the fall of Constantinople. He can make political rulers conform to his wishes by the threat of excommunication. He used his state power to persecute the Protestants. And finally, through his councils and edicts, he has attacked the holy covenant by (1) controverting the plan of salvation by instituting the Eucharist, (2) profaning and replacing Christ's daily sanctuary service, (3) by creating the Rosary, prayers to Mary and the saints, (4) forbidding the reading and possession of the Bible, (5) instituting a system of salvation by works, and (6) finally changing God's commandments by removing the second, allowing for image worship, and replacing the fourth with Sunday worship. The Roman Catholic pope will continue until 1798, when the indignation against him will reach its fill.

37 He shall pay no attention to the gods of his fathers, or to the one beloved by women. He shall not pay attention to any other god, for he shall magnify himself above all.

Parallel text: 17 He shall set his face to come with the strength of his whole kingdom, and he shall bring terms of an agreement and perform them. He shall give him the daughter of women to destroy the kingdom, but it shall not stand or be to his advantage.

- Here we see the Papacy elevating tradition and councils over the Bible, the Word of God, and promoting celibacy. In the mid-sixteenth century, Pope Pius V stated, "The Pope and God are the same, so he has all power in heaven and earth.[50]"

---

[50] quoted in Barclay, Cities Petrus Bertanous Chapter XXVII: 218

- This "god his fathers did not know" refers to traditions, council canons, and Papal Bulls that have come in and replaced the Word of God. A "thus sayeth the Lord" came from an apostle or the Old Testament Scriptures in the early church. Acts 15:21 is clear, *"For from ancient generations Moses (the Torah) has had in every city those who proclaim him, for he is read every Sabbath in the synagogues."*

- While celibacy was a part of the Church dating back to AD 304, in 1074, Pope Gregory VII was the champion of priestly celibacy with his published encyclical forbidding the priests and clergy from marrying and commanded they stay celibate.[51]

38 He shall honor the god of fortresses instead of these. A god whom his fathers did not know he shall honor with gold and silver, with precious stones and costly gifts.

Parallel text: 18 Afterward he shall turn his face to the coastlands and shall capture many of them, but a commander shall put an end to his insolence. Indeed, he shall turn his insolence back upon him.

- This "god of fortresses" can be seen in the pope's temporal power not only with the Jesuits, Dominicans, and the Papal Army but the powers of Catholic nations. Instead of using a "thus sayeth the Lord," the Papacy uses a "thus sayeth the blade."

---

[51] https://www.catholic.org/news/hf/faith/story.php?id=70507

- Pastor and evangelist, Tim Roosenberg gives this description of the "god of fortresses" to include "the cathedrals, which have become their trademark, and the cathedrals have often been used as fortresses during times of war." The god the fathers did not know would be the worship of Mary decorated with gold, precious stones, and pleasant things. Just think of the statues of Mary and how they are decorated.[52]

39 ***He shall deal with the strongest fortresses with the help of a foreign god. Those who acknowledge him he shall load with honor. He shall make them rulers over many and shall divide the land for a price [payment].***

Parallel text: 19 Then he shall turn his face back toward the fortresses of his own land, but he shall stumble and fall, and shall not be found.—He fell in 1798.

- Some see this *"foreign god"* as Mary and her doing the CoRedemtrix with Jesus and believing she was taken to heaven without sin.

- We see this distribution of land for a price in the church's property holdings throughout the world. Also, in AD 1493, Pope Alexander VI issued the Papal Bull *Inter caetera* or "Among other" divided trading and colonizing rights between Portugal and Spain (Castile), excluding other European nations such as England and

---

[52] https://www.islamandchristianity.org/~islama13/study-guides/ DAN_11_2–12_3%20_commentary.pdf

Netherlands. The following year, Spain and Portugal signed the Treaty of Tordesillas. The New World was ripe for Catholic conversion, and the pope declared King Ferdinand of Spain an apostolic vicar in the Indies.

The Pride of the Papacy, Pontifex Maximus—The Greatest Priest

As we did closing the chapter on the Hellenistic Greeks, we will now look at the pride of the Papacy. Recall the verses again in Daniel 11:16–19 paralleled with vv. 36–39, with both instances describing the pride of kings. The Narratives section of Daniel describes another prideful king, Nebuchadnezzar, in Daniel 4. We read there:

> *At the end of twelve months he was walking on the roof of the royal palace of Babylon, and the king answered and said, "Is not this great Babylon, which I have built by my mighty power as a royal residence and for the glory of my majesty?* (Dan. 4:29, 30)

Nebuchadnezzar paid dearly for his pride and arrogance, repented, and was restored to his kingdom. This only happened because of the faithful witness of his servant Daniel and Nebuchadnezzar's heart was open to God's urging. This was not so with the Medieval Papacy. Time and time again, God sent faithful souls to correct the Church, and each time the witnesses were scorned, reviled, and anathematized.

Regarding the title Pontifex Maximus, the Wikipedia entry is revealing to our discussion:

After the Fall of the Eastern Roman Empire with the Fall of Constantinople to the Ottoman Empire and the death of the final Roman emperor Constantine XI in 1453, pontifex maximus became part of the papacy's official titulature of the Bishop of Rome.[53]

CLEMENS XI.
Pontifex Maximus.

Engraving by Christoph Weigel the Elder of Pope Clement XI, giving him the title Pontifex Maximus

---

[53] See also *Oxford Dictionary of the Christian Church* (Oxford University Press 2005 ISBN 978–0–19–280290–3), article Pontifex Maximus

In addition to Pontifex Maximus, the pride of the Popes can be seen in their other official titles:

- Bishop of Rome

- Vicar of Jesus Christ

- Successor of the Prince of the Apostles

- Supreme Pontiff of the Universal Church

- Primate of Italy

- Archbishop and Metropolitan of the Roman Province

- Sovereign of the Vatican City State

- Servant of the servants of God

- His Holiness

- Your Holiness

- Holy Father

- Most Blessed Father

- Most Holy Father

- The Apostolic Lord (used during the medieval period)

6: End-Time Divided Kingdoms

At that time shall arise Michael, the great prince who has charge of your people... your people shall be delivered, everyone whose name shall be found written in the book. —Daniel 12:1

6. End-Time Divided Kingdoms (1798 - 2nd Coming)			
Daniel 2	Daniel 7	Daniel 8-9	Daniel 10-12
			Spiritual Rome attempts to destroy the People of the Covenant

THE FRENCH REVOLUTION left France a majority atheistic power but not completely void of Catholicism and Christianity. There are striking similarities between General Titus and his attitude towards the temple in AD 70 and Napoleon and his attitude towards the pope in 1798. Titus did not want the temple destroyed and gave orders to safeguard it. Napoleon did not want to end the Papacy and even tried to preserve it. An article in *Ministry* magazine entitled, "Napoleon and the Pope—What Really Happened in 1798?"[54] points out

---

[54] https://www.ministrymagazine.org/archive/1979/06/napoleon-and-the-popewhat-really-happenuytreswazXed-in-1798

the France Directory, not Napoleon himself, ordered General Berthier to capture the pope. Hence, we see a parallel with Titus ending the prophecies on Imperial Rome in the legs and Napoleon setting up the prophecies of the End-Time Divided Kingdom. These kingdoms, which we also see in the Toes of Daniel 2, would include the Vatican beginning in 1929.

As head of a Christian church-state system, the Vatican is, in essence, a state founded on a theocratic religious system. The Catholic Church is just one of numerous theocratic state religious systems. The Puritans were not fleeing Catholicism; they fled the Anglican state religion in a Protestant nation. Islam also has a theocratic state system. Essentially, we have a theocratic state religion anytime the majority of religious views begins to suppress minority religious beliefs.

There are also state ideologies based on atheism, or a non-theocratic belief system promoting secularism, evolution, and human reasoning. Often, these secular state ideologies adopt policies prohibiting personal religious views. Prime examples of states who imprisoned, or killed those who would not give up their religious beliefs, include Revolutionary France, Nazi Germany, the Soviet Union, and Communist China.

Protestant America was different. Instead of a state-mandated belief system, the Founders recognized the freedom of individual conscience on these matters. The concept of the separation of church and state was deemed heretical in England and, in 1634, Reverend John Lothropp left the clergy in England to join the Puritans in Massachusetts. He proclaimed that he found a "church without a bishop... and a state without a king." Nevertheless, Reverend Roger Williams began speaking out regarding the Puritans enforcing their religious beliefs by secular law shortly thereafter. Williams was banished from Massachusetts and set up the colony of Rhode Island, where freedom of conscience was respected for all. This ultimately led to placing the separation of church and state front and center in the Bill of Rights as the First Amendment of the U.S. Constitution:

> Congress shall make no law respecting an establishment of religion, or prohibiting the free exercise thereof; or abridging the freedom of speech, or of the press; or the right of the people peaceably to assemble, and to petition the government for a redress of grievances.

This wall of separation, as the U.S. Supreme Court has termed it, is under attack today. The late Cornell University professor and constitutional expert Dr. Milton R. Konvitz wrote extensively on church-state relations in the middle of the last century. In the journal *Law and Contemporary Problems* pf 1949, an article titled "Religion and the State," regarding separation of church and state, Konvitz pens the following:

> The writer... shares the conviction of the Court and of many others that the principle is both wise and sacred, and that it should be protected against any attempt to weaken or limit its power or scope.

Speaking of Founder James Madison, Konvitz writes:

Two score years after his success in the Virginia assembly Madison wrote that any provision for the rights of conscience short of the principle of separation "will be found to leave crevices at least through which bigotry may introduce persecution; a monster that, feeding and thriving on its own venom, gradually swells to a size and strength overwhelming all laws divine and human."

But it does me no injury," he [Madison] wrote in his Notes on Virginia, "for my neighbor to say there are twenty gods, or no God. It neither picks my pocket nor breaks my leg."... "The care of every man's soul belongs to himself."

The small, independent nation of Vatican City, modern-day Christian Rome, has had its sights on America precisely because of this founding principle. From the beginning of the United States, the Papacy has attempted to destroy this principle. Konvitz opens to his readers the "Universal" Church's attitude towards itself and the separation of church and state.

The Catholic Church alone knows what God wants and directs. Religion is not, therefore, an exclusively private affair. There is no freedom, therefore, from "the true religion." There is only free of the true religion as against the state. The state is required to cooperate with the true religion (the Catholic Church).

Pope Leo XIII spoke of "the fatal theory of the separation of church and state." The church is distinct from the state; each has its proper function; but there is no wall of separation between them.

A few years after Leo XIII statements, Pope Pius X, in his 1906 encyclical, condemned the separation of church and state, referencing the prior ecclesiastical authority, which was of the same attitude, stating:

> Hence the Roman Pontiffs have never ceased, as circumstances required, to refute and condemn the doctrine of the separation of Church and State. Our illustrious predecessor, Leo XIII, especially, has frequently and magnificently expounded Catholic teaching on the relations which should subsist between the two societies. "Between them," he says, "there must necessarily be a suitable union, which may not improperly be compared with that existing between body and soul....
>
> That the State must be separated from the Church is a thesis absolutely false, a most pernicious error. Based, as it is, on the principle that the State must not recognize any religious cult, it is in the first place guilty of a great injustice to God; for the Creator of man is also the Founder of human societies, and preserves their existence as He preserves our own. We owe Him, therefore, not only a private cult, but a public and social worship to honor Him.[55]

---

[55] https://www.vatican.va/content/pius-x/en/encyclicals/documents/hf_p-x_enc_11021906_vehementer-nos.html

Thus we can see the clash between the Vatican and America on this issue of freedom of conscience. This is the battleground that the end-time divided kingdoms will struggle over.

The interpretation which follows for Daniel 11:40–45 is based on principles and parallels discussed earlier in this book and will follow a simple, straightforward line of prophecy. There are parts of vv. 40–45 that are clearly interpretable. Still, much of this section is unfulfilled prophecy preventing us from interpreting these future events in graphic detail. However, we can track the course on which the prophecy is heading and recognize the signs as we get closer and closer to Michael standing up to rescue His people, as we see in Daniel 12:1.

Years 1798—Second Coming of Jesus: Vatican Power at the End of Time (vv. 40–45, 12:1)

40 At the time of the end, the king of the south shall attack him, but the king of the north shall rush upon him like a whirlwind, with chariots and horsemen, and with many ships. And he shall come into countries and shall overflow and pass through.

Parallel Text Verse 20:

> *Then shall arise in his place one who shall send an exactor of tribute for the glory of the kingdom. But within a few days he shall be broken, neither in anger nor in battle.*

In 1971, a movie called *The French Connection* was released. Two New York City police detectives end up in France to solve the case of a drug-smuggling ring. In Daniel 11:40, we also find a French connection in our attempt to solve the case of who are the kings of the north and south in v. 40. Follow the chronology on Daniel 11:20 and 40.

> *20 Then shall arise in his* (1st KON—Seleucia) *place one* (2nd KON—Roman Empire) *who shall send an exactor of tribute for the glory of the kingdom.*

> ...

> *40 At the time of the end, the king of the south* (?) *shall attack [or thrust] him* (3rd KON—Medieval Papal States), *but the king of the north* (4th KON—End-Time Rome or the Vatican) *shall rush upon him* (KOS) *like a whirlwind, with chariots and horsemen, and with many ships. And he* (KON—End-Time Rome) *shall come into countries and shall overflow and pass through.*

As discussed previously, the Seleucid kingdom was slowly swallowed up by the Roman Republic, and *"In his place"* came the Roman Empire with their new system of taxation. Verse 20 connects with v. 40 in that Rome, in one form or another, continues until Michael stands up in Daniel 12:1. Recall vv. 20–22 discussing the Roman Empire and vv. 23–39 discussing the Medieval Roman church-state system. Verse 40, like v. 20, initially tells us the previous KON has fallen off the scene, and a new one appears—v. 20 "in his place"—Roman Empire, and v. 40 *"but the King of the North"*—End-Time Rome. One might ask, "How do you know the KON mentioned in the first part of v. 40 is Medieval Rome and not End-Time Rome as we see in the time period?" Context is always king. The "attack" or "thrust" in 1798 was French General Berthier capturing, putting to exile the pope and ending the Medieval Divided Kingdoms. It was after 1798 that the new End-Time Rome began to rise.

Earlier, we looked at v. 23, *"And from the time that an alliance* (Clovis conquering and forcing conversions to Catholicism) *is made with him,"* hence, our first French connection is that France had been in union with the Roman Church since AD 508. That same French kingdom severed that connection by the sword in 1798, ending France's status as "Eldest Daughter of the Church."

A second French connection can be found in secularism. At the same time, France was outlawing Catholicism as their church-state religion, across the ocean, another nation was arising that also forbade Catholicism and all forms of church-state government. Both governments began free of Papal influences; yet over time, Rome began to rebuild and reestablish itself in the politics of both nations. The year 1789 is significant for secularism: first, in the United States, the Constitutional Republic was established based on separation of church and state; next, the Bill of Rights was added to the Constitution, placing religious freedom front and center. In France, the French Revolution began, and a critical statement of political and human rights entitled a "Declaration of the Rights of Man and of the Citizen" was produced. This document was a collaborative effort of the Revolutionary War hero and Frenchman Marquis de Lafayette and Thomas Jefferson. The document placed an emphasis on the principles of human rights and secular natural law and was not based in any way on religious doctrine or authority. The

U.S. Declaration of Independence, its forerunner, also advocated those same principles.

- In 1798, Revolutionary France took Pope Pius VI captive and exiled him, ending the Medieval Divided Kingdoms period and opening the End-Time Divided Kingdoms era. Yet, the weak Papal States lived on until 1870 under the protection of the French. The final collapse came when Napoleon III left the Papacy in Rome to the fate of the Italians.

- The First Vatican Council ended in 1868 as the Franco-Prussian War heated up, and Italian forces moved on the city. Nonetheless, the council did establish the principle of *ex-cathedra, where the Pope has full authority as God on earth in ecclesiastical matters over the universal church.* When the pope speaks in matters of faith or morals, the statements are infallible.

- The temporal Roman Catholicism was resurrected with the Lateran Treaty in 1929 when Italy restored the Papacy's temporal power in the Vatican City. The Vatican received diplomatic relations from nations worldwide, including an ambassador from the United States in 1983. She has been given prominence and universal respect, often being the mouthpiece of Catholic and Protestant churches alike.

- The Second Vatican Council began in 1962 to continue the work of the previous council and ended in 1965. Among other things, this counsel sought to find ways to evangelize not just Europe but the world. Their methods would include ecumenical endeavors with Protestant denominations and interfaith dialogues.

- In the book *Keys of This Blood: Pope John Paul II Versus Russia and the West for Control of the New World Order,* Malachi Martin, an Irish Catholic Priest and ex-Jesuit, detailed the relationship between Pope John Paul II and President Ronald Reagan in the overthrow of Communism in Europe. Martin writes, on page 14, "Willing or not, ready or not, we are all involved in an all-out, no-holds-barred, three-way global competition." And on page 17, "The competition is about who will establish the first one-world system of government that has ever existed in the society of nations. It is not too much to say, in fact, that the chosen purpose of John Paul's pontificate... is to be the victor in that competition, now well under way."[56] Some write off Martin's work as fiction, yet he held a unique, behind-the-scenes perspective on the activities of the Vatican during this time, which few before him have voiced, and much of his predictions have rung true.

- The pattern over time, starting with President Reagan, shows an ever-increasing relationship and cooperation between the Vatican and the United States. This path is leading to a combining of powers to reinforce

---

[56] https://www.ministrymagazine.org/archive/1991/06/the-keys-of-this-blood

the Catholic Church's dogmas, just as was seen in the Medieval Period.

- Detailed Interpretation:

  At the time of the end (after 1798), *the king of the south* (France, then Italy) *shall attack him* (Papacy and Papal States), *but the king of the north* (Papacy and Vatican) *shall rush upon him like a whirlwind,* with (symbolic) *chariots and horsemen, and with many ships* (Vatican I, II). *And he shall come into countries* (with ecumenicism) *and shall overflow and pass through* (an example was the union between the Papacy and the West to take down communism in Europe).

With these French connections in mind, it is easy to see how "At the time of the end" or 1798, "the king of the south" or secularism found in both the United States and France "shall attack him" by capturing the Pope and setting up secular governments void of the oppressive church-state policies found in the Medieval Anglican and Catholic church-state systems.

41 He shall come into the glorious land. And tens of thousands shall fall, but these shall be delivered out of his hand: Edom and Moab and the main part of the Ammonites.

Parallel Text Verse 21a:

  21a In his place shall arise a contemptible person to whom royal majesty has not been given.

- In 2015, we witnessed Pope Francis standing in the well of the U.S. Congress, and subsequently, the next day gave an address to the world at the United Nations. While this may or may not be the exact fulfillment of the prophecy regarding the Papacy coming with power into Protestant lands, it is apparent where the path is headed in regard to a union of the Christian church and state.

- Edom, Moab, and the Ammonites were ancient relatives of the Jews. In the final days, when the full intentions of the Vatican will be revealed, many from the various Protestant churches will come out and take their stand on God's side.

42 He shall stretch out his hand against the countries, and the land of Egypt shall not escape.

Parallel Text Verse 21b:

> *He shall come in without warning*

- Recall reading back in v. 31, "*Forces from him shall appear and profane the temple and fortress, and shall take away the regular* (temple ministry). *And they shall set up the abomination that makes desolate.*" During the Medieval period, the Papacy had used its power to enforce its dogmas on non-Catholics.

- As was done during the Medieval Divided Kingdoms period, the Vatican, with the leaders of the United

States and the nations of the world, will work hand in hand to force the inhabitants to keep certain tenets of the Catholic Church.

43 He shall become ruler of the treasures of gold and of silver, and all the precious things of Egypt, and the Libyans and the Cushites shall follow in his train.

Parallel Text Verse 21c:

> *and obtain the kingdom by flatteries.*

- Vatican authority and power will sweep the world over, including secular environmentalists, atheists, pagans, Wiccans, and even those in Islam and Eastern religions, etc.

44 But news from the east and the north shall alarm him, and he shall go out with great fury to destroy and devote many to destruction.

Parallel Text Verse 22b:

> *22a Armies shall be utterly swept away before him and broken,*

- The loud cry of the authentic scriptural covenant message pressing all inhabitants to choose between standing with God and His people or standing with the counterfeit mark and traditions of the Catholic Church. God's people will keep His Ten Commandments and hold to the Bible alone as their authority.

Here, let us pause our interpretation to interject a scenario from the narrative section of the book of Daniel. In chapter 3, we see Daniel's three friends, Shadrack, Meshack, and Abednego. The three Hebrews had observed the image being built for quite some time, they knew what was coming down the line, and the young men even went and stood before the image. It was not until the command to worship that our heroes refused to obey. Certainly, other Jews in the crowd noticed their sandals needing lashing at that very moment. Still, others probably went along with the crowd, bending down, not wanting to make a scene. News of the three Hebrews' willful rejection of the command to bow and worship enraged King Nebuchadnezzar. First, he pleads with them to comply, yet the Hebrews stand firm, having the truth of God settled in their minds. Nebuchadnezzar's rage returns and demands the destruction of the Hebrews, yet Jesus miraculously saves them in the fire.

We can see a scenario playing out just like this in our day. The Christian church-state union will enact a law forcing worship contrary to the law of God. The faithful servants of God will go as far as possible but will inevitably stand and say as our Hebrew servants:

> *[W]e have no need to answer you in this matter. If this be so, our God whom we serve is able to deliver us from the burning fiery furnace, and he will deliver us out of your hand, O king. But if not, be it known to you, O king, that we will not serve your gods or worship the golden image that you have set up.* (Dan. 3:17–18)

45 And he shall pitch his palatial tents between the sea and the glorious holy mountain. Yet he shall come to his end, with none to help him.

Parallel Text Verse 22b:

> *even the prince of the covenant (will be utterly swept away and broken)*—Contrast to death decree on the people of the covenant.

- The *"sea"* here are the peoples of the earth.

  o Daniel 7:3, *"And four great beasts came up out of the* **sea***, different from one another."*—they all came from population centers.

  o Isaiah 60:5, *"Then you shall see and be radiant; your heart shall thrill and exult, because the abundance of the* **sea** *shall be turned to you, the wealth of the nations shall come to you."*—the context is the peoples of nations.

  o Revelation 17:15, *"And the angel said to me, 'The* **waters** *that you saw, where the prostitute is seated, are peoples and multitudes and nations and languages'"*— waters and sea are synonymous.

- A "mountain" often represents God's kingdom. As mentioned earlier in chapter 4, this "glorious holy mountain" is Jesus's kingdom and His redeemed people. We saw this same mountain in Daniel 2:35, where we read, *"But the stone that struck the image became a great mountain and filled the whole earth."*

- Enraged, the Vatican will coerce the United States and the world to pass a death decree against Michael's people—all who hold to the Bible and God's commandments.

- As in the time of Esther, just before the execution date for the decree to be enforced, the Vatican, as did evil Haman, will come to its end. Yet, the law cannot be changed, and even though the key adversary is gone, God's people will still have to fight, yet it will be through the strength of the Holy Spirit.

Now, we need a second pause in our interpretation, this time to look at Daniel 6. Rival administrators have bitter hate for Daniel, yet no charge or blemish could be found on his record. So, a trap was set to get the faithful servant of God. The new law was intended to force him to choose to follow the world and live or stick to his daily worship custom and die. The administrators were so sure Daniel would not alter his worship routine that they just watched and waited:

> *All the high officials of the kingdom, the prefects and the satraps, the counselors and the governors are agreed that the king should establish an ordinance and enforce an injunction, that whoever makes petition to any god or man for thirty days, except to you, O king, shall be cast into the den of lions.* (Dan. 6:7)

Again, we can see this scenario playing out. Infuriated, the people will demand a law to force compliance on pain of death. Yet, God's end-time servants will continue their worship customs as Daniel did over 2,500 years before.

> *When Daniel knew that the document had been signed, he went to his house where he had windows in his upper chamber open toward Jerusalem. He got down on his knees three times a day and prayed and gave thanks before his God, as he had done previously.* (Dan. 6:10)

As the forces of the church-state union converge on God's people for violation of their man-made law, God intervenes and saves His people.

Daniel 12:1 is the conclusion of the prophecy of Chapter 11

> *At that time shall arise Michael, the great prince who has charge of your people. And there shall be a time of trouble, such as never has been since there was a nation till that time. But at that time your people shall be delivered, everyone whose name shall be found written in the book.*

7. God's Eternal Kingdom
Daniel 2   Daniel 7   Daniel 8-9   Daniel 10-12
                                      Michael Delivers God's People

Who *is* this Michael of Daniel 10–12?

As a heavenly being, Michael is mentioned three times in Daniel's vision in chapters 10–12. He is also mentioned twice in the New Testament, once in Jude 9 where he is disputing with Satan over the resurrection of Moses to heaven, and the other is in Revelation 12, where he is commanding the war in heaven against Satan with his angels.

There are three views on who Michael is. The first is where Michael is the highest, or Archangel (Jude 9), and one of the chief princes (Dan. 10:13), with Gabriel being subordinate to Him. The second view is where Michael is Jesus, a created being, and is the brother of Lucifer. Lucifer rebelled, and the Father sent Michael or Jesus to die on the cross and defeat Lucifer there. The third position is where Michael is the pre-incarnate Jesus, one with the Father before the incarnation and one fully God and fully man.

Michael appears in Scripture to do more than any mere angel, so the first view seems to be flawed. Jesus was not a created being or the brother of the angel Lucifer, so the second view is obviously unscriptural. Outlined below are the justifications for the third position:

1. The name Michael in Hebrew means "who is like God." No one other than Jesus is like God the Father. John 10:30: *"I and the Father are one."*

2. The word *Archangel* is from two words, *arch* meaning "chief" and *angel* meaning "messenger." John states in 1:1–2, *"In the beginning was the Word, and the Word was*

with God, and the Word was God. He was in the beginning with God."

From Strong's Definition:

"λόγος lógos, log'-os; from G3004; something said (including the thought); by implication, a topic (subject of discourse), also reasoning (the mental faculty) or motive; by extension, a computation; specially, (with the article in John) the Divine Expression (i.e. Christ):—account, cause, communication."

Here we see Jesus's role in the Godhead as the chief messenger to both angels and humanity. He arises and delivers God's people.

3. In Daniel 10:13, the angel Gabriel could not influence the king of Persia because Satan was manipulating the king. Michael had to come and influence the king of Persia. As the highest angel can influence humans, Gabriel is tasked with vital messages to give to humans like Daniel (Dan. 8:16; 9:20–21) and Mary, the mother of Jesus (Luke 1:19). Yet, he has no power against Satan. Hebrews 1:14 *"Are they (angels) not all ministering spirits sent out to serve for the sake of those who are to inherit salvation?"*

4. Young's Literal Translation Bible (YLT) translates the phrase in Daniel 10:13b as *"Michael, first of the chief heads"* instead of *"one of the chief princes."* Jesus is the commander-in-chief or head of the angelic force. We

see this in Matthew 13:41, *"The Son of Man (Jesus) will send his angels."*

5. In both New Testament passages, Michael is fighting Satan. Only Jesus can defeat Satan. Hebrews 1:1–15,

[H]e (Jesus) *himself likewise partook of the same things, that through death he might destroy the one who has the power of death, that is, the devil, and deliver all those who through fear of death were subject to lifelong slavery.*

6. In Revelation 12, Michael fights and defeats Satan. He threw him out of heaven. Jesus plainly states in Luke 10:18, *"And he said to them, 'I saw Satan fall like lightning from heaven.'"*

7. The statement in Daniel 12:1, *"At that time shall arise Michael,"* or as the YLT translates it, *"And at that time stand up doth Michael."* The book of Daniel is about judgment. This is precisely what happens at the end of the prophecy in chapter 7. During a criminal trial, the judge sits while he or she listens to arguments from both sides. At the end of a court session, the judge makes his decision and stands up, signifying the judgment is over, and the decision is made. In Daniel 12, Michael has made his judgment against the King of the North and for His people, so he stands. Jesus said in John 5:22, *"For the Father judgeth no man, but hath committed all judgment unto the Son."* Judgment is never given to a mere angel; therefore, Michael here must be Jesus. We can see this in the narrative of Acts 7 and the stoning of Stephan.

Stephan has a vision while they are stoning him. Acts 7:56 states, *"And he said, "Behold, I see the heavens opened, and the Son of Man standing at the right hand of God."* Jesus has judged the Jewish nation, found them guilty, and has stood up.

For a final note on Michael, we turn to Matthew Henry, a Presbyterian minister and biblical scholar of the seventeenth century, who wrote this regarding Michael as the incarnate Jesus:

> When Christ appears he will recompense tribulation to those that trouble his people. There shall be a time of trouble, threatening to all, but ruining to all the implacable enemies of God's kingdom among men, such trouble as never was since there was a nation. This is applicable.

1. To the destruction of Jerusalem, which Christ calls (perhaps with an eye to this prediction) such a great tribulation as was not since the beginning of the world to this time, Mt. 24:21. This the angel had spoken much of (ch. 9:26, 27); and it happened about the same time that Christ set up the gospel-kingdom in the world, that Michael our prince stands up. Or,

2. To the judgment of the great day, that day that shall burn as an oven, and consume the proud and all that do

wickedly; that will be such a day of trouble as never was to all those whom Michael our prince stands against.[57]

- Probation closed on the Jewish nation in 34AD with the stoning of Stephan, and Jesus standing up, pronounced the Jewish nation "guilty," closing the court case in God vs. the Jewish nation (see Acts 7). When this final death decree falls on God's people, probation closes. Michael or Jesus will stand up, pronounce the Christian church-state system led by the Vatican "guilty," and close the court case in God vs. the Vatican and her church-state system, giving judgment in favor of God's covenant keeping people.

- It cannot be overstated that we are not speaking of sincere members of the Catholic Church. We are speaking of the church-state system and the Vatican hierarchy. Jesus clearly states in John 10:14–16,

I am the good shepherd. I know my own and my own know me, just as the Father knows me and I know the Father; and I lay down my life for the sheep. And I have other sheep that are not of this fold. I must bring them also, and they will listen to my voice. So there will be one flock, one shepherd.

In the previous prophecies of Daniel 2, 7, and 8, we see a similar ending to this great conflict, and God's people of all ages enter His eternal kingdom.

---

[57] Matthew Henry, "An Exposition, with Practical Observations, of the Book of the Prophet Daniel," in An Exposition of the Old and New Testament, v 4, p. 869.

- Daniel 2:44–45, *"And in the days of those kings the God of heaven will set up a kingdom that shall never be destroyed, nor shall the kingdom be left to another people. It shall break in pieces all these kingdoms and bring them to an end, and it shall stand forever, just as you saw that a stone was cut from a mountain by no human hand, and that it broke in pieces the iron, the bronze, the clay, the silver, and the gold."*

- Daniel 7:26–27, *"But the court shall sit in judgment, and his dominion shall be taken away, to be consumed and destroyed to the end. And the kingdom and the dominion and the greatness of the kingdoms under the whole heaven shall be given to the people of the saints of the Most High; his kingdom shall be an everlasting kingdom, and all dominions shall serve and obey him."*

- Daniel 8:25, *"By his cunning he shall make deceit prosper under his hand, and in his own mind he shall become great. Without warning he shall destroy many. And he shall even rise up against the Prince of princes, and he shall be broken— but by no human hand."*

Conclusion

"And those who are wise shall shine like the brightness of the sky above; and those who turn many to righteousness, like the stars forever and ever." — Daniel 12:3

Here, again, is the division of kingdoms found in Daniel 11:

Verse(s)	Empire/Power
11:2	Medo-Persia Empire with freedom of religion for all, albeit polytheistic worship
11:3–19	Greek Empire with Hellenistic Dynasties of the Seleucids and Ptolemies
11:20–22	Imperial Roman Empire with the church-state union in the Sanhedrin and Governor Pilate
11:23–39	Medieval Divided Kingdoms with church-state systems found in Rome and Constantinople
11:40–45	End-Time Divided Kingdoms with the church-state union in the Vatican and the United States
12:1	Michael's Kingdom with freedom of religion, yet all will *freely choose* to worship of the God of Heaven

Stages of Prophetic History

1. Babylonian Empire (605 - 539BC)

Daniel 2	Daniel 7	Daniel 8-9	Daniel 10-12
		N/A	N/A

2. Medo-Persian Empire (539 - 331BC)

Daniel 2	Daniel 7	Daniel 8-9	Daniel 10-12
			Cyrus Delivers God's People

3. Greek Empire (331 - 31BC)

Daniel 2	Daniel 7	Daniel 8-9	Daniel 10-12
			KON - Seleucid Dynasty KOS - Ptolemaic Dynasty

4. Roman Empire (31BC - 476 AD)

Daniel 2	Daniel 7	Daniel 8-9	Daniel 10-12
			Imperial Rome arises and destroys the Prince of the Covenant

5. Medieval Divided Kingdoms (476 - 1798)

Daniel 2	Daniel 7	Daniel 8-9	Daniel 10-12
			KON – Rome Church-State Union KOS – Constantinople Church-State Union

6. End-Time Divided Kingdoms (1798 - 2nd Coming)

Daniel 2	Daniel 7	Daniel 8-9	Daniel 10-12
			Spiritual Rome attempts to destroy the People of the Covenant

7. God's Eternal Kingdom

Daniel 2	Daniel 7	Daniel 8-9	Daniel 10-12
			Michael Delivers God's People

This interpretation does many things other interpretations do not. First, it gives a prophetic understanding in a clear, concise, systematic manner that is chronological and literal. Next, it enlarges and expands the prophecies of 2, 7, and 8–9. Still, it does not add elements that were not seen in the earlier prophecies. Finally, it has a specific message of warning for those of us living in the last days: Beware of the coming church and state union, which will cause great conflict, not only in the nations of the world but, moreover, to God's faithful people. This should give us confidence and enthusiasm in sharing the message of Danial 11.

It was never my intention to bring another position to Daniel 11. My purpose was simply to study Daniel's prophecies for myself and then make a different type of Bible study emphasizing each kingdom and what each of the four prophecies said about that kingdom instead of our usual chapter by chapter studies. My study was going to be titled "Daniel from a Different Direction," yet it turned into something much more. While loving the study of the Bible and history, I feel that I am just an amateur in the areas of theology and history. Innumerable hours of diligent study and research have gone into this book, and to be honest, I cannot explain some of the insights and concepts in this position other than God put them into my mind as I prayed and studied over these issues. It was only the Lord who could have done this.

I firmly believe we are at the tips of the toenails of Daniel's image, and the closing scenes will be rapid ones. The New Testament complement of the Book of Daniel states, *"He which testifieth these things saith, Surely I come quickly. Amen. Even so, come, Lord Jesus. The grace of our Lord Jesus Christ be with you all. Amen"* (Rev. 22:20–21).

I want to reemphasize something that I discussed earlier regarding our duty as priests of Jesus. God's New Testament people are a "holy and royal priesthood" of believers (1 Peter 2:9).

Symbolically in the Courtyard, we are justified and have:

(1) accepted Jesus who was sacrificed once for all, and

(2) been baptized into His death and resurrection.

We are now able to enter the Holy Place of the Sanctuary and spiritually perform the "continual/daily" duties of a New Testament priest:

(3) before the Altar of Incense with our personal and corporate prayers,

(4) before the Table of Showbread through Bible study and devotions, and

(5) before the Lampstand, letting our light shine through our Fruit of the Spirit and our Gift(s) of the Spirit.

Finally, we are ministers at the curtain separating the Holy from the Most Holy place

(6) symbolically sprinkling the blood of Jesus by trusting in His merits as our only Sacrifice and High Priest to

provide us mercy and give us the strength to keep His commandments. Thus, we emulate His character of love in our lives. Moreover, we are being prepared for glorification at His soon coming.

Whether one accepts the interpretation brought forward in this book or not, it is hard to ignore the monumental events and transformation our world has made just in the last twenty years. Many are looking for the imminent return of Jesus, yet how will we know if we are ready? I am convinced we will not be prepared unless we are studying the Bible for ourselves, praying earnestly, and sharing the love of Jesus through our fruit of the Spirit and gifts from the Holy Spirit.

Now is the time for us to be doing our daily priestly duties in the sanctuary by praying, studying, and letting our light shine. Even so, let it be said of us,

> *And* _____ (insert your name) *who is wise shall shine like the brightness of the sky above by reflecting the character of Jesus; and he/she will turn many to righteousness, like the stars forever and ever.* (Dan. 12:3 paraphrased)

Appendix A:
A verse by verse
Interpretation of Daniel 11

Introduction

1 And as for me, in the first year of Darius the Mede, I stood up to confirm and strengthen him.

> The verse is part of the long introduction we find in Daniel 10. The angel Gabriel is speaking here. Persian king Cyrus has defeated Babylonian King Nabonidus at the Battle of Opis on the Tigris River and his son, Coregent Belshazzar, in Babylon. Darius the Mede was the initial ruler of the province of Babylon but almost certainly died soon after the capture.

Years of 539–465 BC: Persia (v. 2)

2 And now I will show you the truth. Behold, three more kings shall arise in Persia, and a fourth shall be far richer than all of them. And when he has become strong through his riches, he shall stir up all against the kingdom of Greece.

- 4 Persian Kings

  - Cyrus the Great 559–530 BC

  - Cambyses II 530–522 BC

  - Darius I 522–486 BC

  - Xerxes I 485–465 BC

- This rich, powerful fourth king is Xerxes I (the Greek name for Ahasuerus), Queen Esther's husband; he raised a huge army from forty nations and attacked Greece around 490 and 480 BC.

- The Greek city-states began to band together to repel the Persian invasion.

Years of 331–301 BC: Greece and Alexander (vv. 3–4)

3 Then a mighty king shall arise, who shall rule with great dominion and do as he wills.

- Alexander and the Grecian Empire

4 And as soon as he has arisen, his kingdom shall be broken and divided toward the four winds of heaven, but not to his posterity, nor according to the authority with which he ruled, for his kingdom shall be plucked up and go to others besides these.

- On June 10 or 11, 323 BC, in Babylon, Alexander died of malaria or typhoid fever combined with a drinking binge.

- "divided to the four winds" between his generals in 301 BC at the Battle of Ipsus.

  o North—Lysimachus eastward in Thrace and Asia Minor

  o South—Ptolemy in Egypt and southern section of Asia Minor

  o East—Seleucus to the Indus River

  o West—Cassander in Macedonia and Greece

- "not to his posterity" for twenty-five years, Alexander's half-brother tried to keep the divisions together, but Alexander's only son and his Persian mother were poisoned in ca 310 BC by Cassander, son of Antipater, regent of Macedonia.

Years of 301–188 BC: Hellenistic Seleucid and Ptolemy Dynasties (vv. 5–19)

5 "Then the king of the south shall be strong, but one of his princes shall be stronger than he and shall rule, and his authority shall be a great authority.

- *"King of the South"* located to the south of Palestine is Ptolemy I (Sotor) assisted *"one of the princes"* Seleucus I (Nicator) to regain the territories of Mesopotamia ca 312 BC and became a greater ruler than Ptolemy I ca 281 BC.

6 After some years they shall make an alliance, and the daughter of the king of the south shall come to the king of the north to make an agreement. But she shall not retain the strength of her arm, and he and his arm shall not endure, but she shall be given up, and her attendants, he who fathered her, and he who supported her in those times.

- *"King of the North,"* located north of Palestine, is now Antiochus II (Theos), in ca 253 BC, who marries Bernice, the daughter of Ptolemy II (Philadelphus). They have a son, but separate, and Antiochus II reconciles with his other wife and sister, Laodice. Antiochus II dies suddenly, possibly by Laodice, who also Bernice and her son had killed along with her Egyptian attendants.

7 And from a branch from her roots one shall arise in his place. He shall come against the army and enter the fortress of the king of the north, and he shall deal with them and shall prevail.

- In ca 246 BC Ptolemy III (Euergetes) invaded Syria in revenge for his sister Bernice and was victorious all the way to Mesopotamia and established Egyptian sea power along the eastern coast of the Mediterranean Sea, but he was defeated at the Battle of Andros near the Aegean islands in 246 BC.

8 He shall also carry off to Egypt their gods with their metal images and their precious vessels of silver and gold, and for some years he shall refrain from attacking the king of the north.

- In ca 239 BC Ptolemy III brought back enormous amounts of Egyptian treasures looted by the Persians but did not attack the Seleucid empire again.

9 Then the latter shall come into the realm of the king of the south but shall return to his own land.

- Seleucus II tried to march against Ptolemy III in 240 BC and regain the wealth lost but was defeated and turned back.

10 His sons shall wage war and assemble a multitude of great forces, which shall keep coming and overflow and pass through, and again shall carry the war as far as his fortress.

- The "sons" of Seleucus II, Seleucus III and Antiochus III, would carry on the war against Ptolemy IV (Philopater) in the Palestine region. In 219 BC Antiochus III marched to the "fortress" of Seleucia or port of Antioch on the Mediterranean sea.

11 Then the king of the south, moved with rage, shall come out and fight against the king of the north. And he shall raise a great multitude, but it shall be given into his hand.

- In 217 BC, at the Battle of Raphia, Ptolemy IV met Antiochus III, each with huge armies of around 60,000 infantry, 6,000 cavalry members, 100 elephants. Ptolemy IV soundly defeated Antiochus III.

12 And when the multitude is taken away, his heart shall be exalted, and he shall cast down tens of thousands, but he shall not prevail.

- After Ptolemy IV defeated Antiochus III at the Battle of Raphia, he instituted the Raphia Decree, placing himself on the level of the ancient pharaohs, making himself a god, he put down the Egyptian Revolts, and finally, in 204 BC, Ptolemy IV died of unclear circumstances.

13 For the king of the north shall again raise a multitude, greater than the first. And after some years he shall come on with a great army and abundant supplies.

- In 201 BC, Antiochus III invaded Palestine again. "*After some years*" refers to the sixteen years between the Battle of Raphia and his second invasion which gave him time to amass a great army and supplies.

14 In those times many shall rise against the king of the south, and the violent among your own people shall lift themselves up in order to fulfill the vision, but they shall fail.

- Ptolemy IV goes home triumphant, but he begins having problems on the home front. During this time, Ptolemy also had several revolts in his kingdom from native Egyptians over their dissatisfaction with the Egyptian priesthood and political murders. All these constituted a *"rise against the king of the south."*

- The *"violent among your own people"* are Jews who mixed religious and political power in a single person and committed aggressive acts against census-taking and taxation, beginning with Ptolemy III. Moreover, they constructed a "vision" for an independent state of Judah. Yet, the calamities that befell the Hellenistic Jews due to these revolts and the plain statement that the vision *"shall fail"* is a good indication that God was not with them in this.

15 Then the king of the north shall come and throw up siegeworks and take a well-fortified city. And the forces of the south shall not stand, or even his best troops, for there shall be no strength to stand.

- Antiochus III captured Gaza from Ptolemy V in 201 BC and captured Sidon, making the Egyptian army surrender at the Battle of Panium in 200 BC, ending Ptolemaic control of Palestine.

16 But he who comes against him shall do as he wills, and none shall stand before him. And he shall stand in the glorious land, with destruction in his hand.

- *"shall do as he wills"* the Romans—who came against Antiochus III—shall do as he wills, and none shall stand before Rome. And Antiochus III shall stand in the glorious land, with destruction in his hand.

17 He shall set his face to come with the strength of his whole kingdom, and he shall bring terms of an agreement and perform them. He shall give him the daughter of women to destroy the kingdom, but it shall not stand or be to his advantage.

- In trying to conquer Egypt, Antiochus III (King of the North) made an agreement with the young Ptolemy V (King of the South), which included giving Antiochus's daughter Cleopatra I in marriage to Ptolemy V in Egypt. Cleopatra I turned against her father and gave up all ties to her ancestry in the Seleucid dynasty and later became the queen of Egypt and adopted the Ptolemy dynasty as her own.

18 Afterward he shall turn his face to the coastlands and shall capture many of them, but a commander shall put an end to his insolence. Indeed, he shall turn his insolence back upon him.

- Antiochus III Magnus turned against Asia Minor but was turned back by the Roman general Lucius Cornelius Scipio in 190 BC. In 188 BC, Antiochus III was forced to sign the Treaty of Apamea. *Both* he and Ptolemy V lost all claims to lands Asia Minor.

19 Then he shall turn his face back toward the fortresses of his own land, but he shall stumble and fall, and shall not be found.

- Antiochus III was killed while trying to plunder a pagan temple near Susa (187 BC), just a year following the peace accords with Rome in 188 BC; thus, he stumbled and fell and was found no more. Rome is now the dominating power and has subdued both the KON and the KOS in the Treaty of Apamea in 188 BC.

Years of 31 BC–AD 70: Imperial Roman Empire (vv. 20–22)

20 Then shall arise in his place one who shall send an exactor of tribute for the glory of the kingdom. But within a few days he shall be broken, neither in anger nor in battle.

- Augustus instituted efficient taxation and census-taking system, using the funds for elaborate architecture, and expanded the network of Roman roads leading to the expression, "All roads lead to Rome." On these roads, the gospel spread to all parts of the world.

- On August 19, AD 14, near Naples, Italy, Caesar Augustus died after some months of declining health neither in "anger nor in battle."

21 In his place shall arise a contemptible person to whom royal majesty has not been given. He shall come in without warning and obtain the kingdom by flatteries.

- Tiberius Caesar was in power at the time of Jesus's crucifixion thirty-three years later. Though a great military commander, he spurned court life and politics. Augustus attempted to groom his nephew, then a grandson, and still another adopted son for the throne. Each died before Augustus, leaving only Tiberius, the bottom of the barrel, left for the throne.

- Tiberius was initially a good ruler, but after the death of his son, he soon fell out of favor with the people. He became eccentric, aloof, and reclusive. He would leave the city to ruthless leaders who abused the people while he went off to the paradise island of Capri and committed numerous sexual debaucheries. Tiberius dies a lonely, old man in 37 AD.

22 Armies shall be utterly swept away before him and broken, even the prince of the covenant.

- First, we have a political statement: *"Armies shall be broken and utterly swept away before him* (or the Roman army).*"*

- Then, we have a religious statement: *"The prince of the covenant shall be broken and utterly swept away before him* (or Rome).*"*

- This text is unquestionably about the power of Rome through its crushing legions, not only devouring nations around them but, more importantly, being the power who through Pilate issued a death decree and carried it out on Jesus, the prince of the covenant. Even so, the Gospel of Salvation—through a condemned and executed innocent man—spread like wildfire to all the nations of the world.

Years of AD 508–ca AD 1215: Establishment of Church-State System in Europe (vv. 23–31)

23 And from the time that an alliance is made with him he shall act deceitfully, and he shall become strong with a small people.

- Starting at AD 476, after the fall of the Western Roman Empire, the Papacy had to make temporary alliances with its barbarian neighbors in order to survive. The alliance with the Franks beginning in AD 508 would not only be stronger than all the rest but would remain steadfast until the time appointed of 1798.

- At this time, because of the barbarian invasions and Arianism, Catholicism was small but began to spread rapidly throughout southern, central, and western Europe through missionaries and with the sword of the Franks.

24 Without warning he shall come into the richest parts of the province, and he shall do what neither his fathers nor his fathers' fathers have done, scattering among them plunder, spoil, and goods. He shall devise plans against strongholds, but only for a time.

- In AD 533, the Papacy began the process of receiving a temporal dominion with the Byzantine Emperor giving the pope the city of Rome.

- Simony, the practice of buying and selling ecclesiastical privileges, church offices, or promotion, began as early as AD 498.

- The pope of Rome had to *"devise plans"* to be a temporal ruler, using monastic establishments to spread spiritual rule throughout Europe and leverage against the emperor who had the Bishop of Constantinople at his side.

- *"But only for a time"* is a significant phrase. The word *time* means "the time of an event." And the Papacy would engage in scattering plunder, spoil, and goods among those who honor them until the time of the end in 1798.

25 And he shall stir up his power and his heart against the king of the south with a great army. And the king of the south shall wage war with an exceedingly great and mighty army, but he shall not stand, for plots shall be devised against him.

- From AD 535–554 the Gothic Wars with Byzantine General Narses (KOS) and an overwhelming force defeated the Ostrogoths, again liberating Rome at the Battle of Taginae of AD 552 and vanquishing the remaining Ostrogothic army for good.

- As to *"plots shall be devised against him,"* this can clearly be seen in the fact that Papacy initially supported the Arian Ostrogoths and in the subsequent interplay between the popes, Ostrogoths, and the emperor.

26 Even those who eat his food shall break him. His army shall be swept away, and many shall fall down slain.

- None of the alliances with the barbarian nation could give the Papacy the temporal power against Constantinople during this period. The Exarchate of Ravenna, under the authority of the Byzantine Emperor, dominated the region. The populace of the peninsula had been devastated by war, famine, and disease. Also, the Papacy had lost control over Papal elections. The Papacy would not gain the upper hand on Constantinople until 800 with the crowning of the French king, Charlemagne.

27 And as for the two kings, their hearts shall be bent on doing evil. They shall speak lies at the same table, but to no avail, for the end is yet to be at the time appointed.

- In AD 711 Pope Constantine traveled to Constantinople to end a dispute over the Quinisext Ecumenical Council with Emperor Justinian II. However, the pope's real motive was the split over sacramental marriages. A compromise was reached where Pope Constantine gave ground on "Economia" or the handling, management, and disposition, of the council, but he held firm on most Papal concerns. It was truly a compromise borne in diplomatic speak between the two rival "kings" where many words were spoken but accomplished little towards ending the rift between the two parties.

28 And he shall return to his land with great wealth, but his heart shall be set against the holy covenant. And he shall work his will and return to his own land.

- After AD 756 and the establishment of the Papal States, territories in the majority of the Italian Peninsula gave direct temporal sovereign rule to the Pope.

- In AD 787, the Second Council of Nicaea approved idol worship and declared that tradition superseded Scripture.

29 At the time appointed he shall return and come into the south, but it shall not be this time as it was before.

- The pope, as KON with his Frankish armies, attacked Constantinople, the KOS again. Charlemagne, with sizable force, attacked the Byzantine peripheral states of Venice and the Dalmatian coast. The Byzantines were not in a position to send a force to their aid. Additionally, the pope refused to acknowledge Irene as Byzantine Emperor in AD 797. In AD 811, a peace treaty was finally signed between Charlemagne and Byzantine Emperor Michael I, where the Byzantine Empire would accept Charlemagne as king of the Franks, and Charlemagne would give back the Dalmatian coast region.

30 For ships of Kittim shall come against him, and he shall be afraid and withdraw, and shall turn back and be enraged and take action against the holy covenant. He shall turn back and pay attention to those who forsake the holy covenant.

- Out of their Mediterranean Sea bases, Arab pirate raiders sacked Rome in AD 843, which caused the Papacy to withdraw and form the Italian League of

Papal, Neapolitan, Amalfitan, and Gaetan ships to fend off the Arab pirates and won the famous naval Battle of Ostia in AD 849.

- In AD 870, at the Fourth Council of Constantinople, the covenant was again attacked with the sanctioning of idolatry and the veneration of Mary.

31 Forces from him shall appear and profane the temple and fortress, and shall take away the regular burnt offering. And they shall set up the abomination that makes desolate.

- At this point in time, the Papacy held all ecclesiastical authority in the Western Church. The pope's *"forces"* were the temporal powers in Europe, the increased focus of the Inquisition beginning in the 1250s and later with the Jesuit Order beginning in 1540

- At the Fourth Council of Lateran in 1215, it was ordered that parishioners must keep the annual reception of penance and the Eucharist. They also used the term *transubstantiation* to explain the real presence of Christ in the Eucharist. Through the Eucharist and the sacraments, the Catholic Church has removed the daily/continual sanctuary ministries of lay members. Congregants no longer study the Bible for themselves, pray directly to God, or witness to their neighbors.

- In AD 70, the Imperial Roman flags or standards with the iconic eagle were set up in the temple of Jerusalem commemorating their victory, which was the abomination prophesied in AD 31 by Jesus. Likewise, starting around 1215 with the sanctions of its counsels, the Papacy harnessed the use of secular forces to enforce the Church dogmas, which were in direct contradiction to the teachings of the Apostles and of Scripture, especially in the areas of the sanctuary which set up the Papal Roman abomination of desolation.

Years of ca 1215—1798: Protestant Reformation (vv. 32–35)

32 He shall seduce with flattery those who violate the covenant, but the people who know their God shall stand firm and take action

- Those who violate the covenant are those who choose to accept tradition and Church dogma over Scripture.

- This "flattery" or smooth things can be seen in the praise of the Mass in the Roman Missal, which was produced in AD 1570 and continued in use unchanged for 400 years.

- The Catholic Church worked hand in hand with the Habsburg Dynasty against the Protestant Reformation overtly in Spain and Italy and covertly used the Jesuits in Central Europe.

- Shortly after the Third Council of Lateran, in 1209, the French military began the Albigensian or Cather Crusade, which lasted for twenty years.

33 And the wise among the people shall make many understand, though for some days they shall stumble by sword and flame, by captivity and plunder.

- In 1553, Queen Mary I, or "Bloody Mary," took the English throne, and many Protestants were exiled, imprisoned, burned at the stake, tortured, or punished in other ways. "Foxe's Book of Martyrs" records many accounts of persecution.

34 When they stumble, they shall receive a little help. And many shall join themselves to them with flattery,

- Many Catholic sympathizers in Protestant areas joined with the Protestants to avoid conflict. With the full authority of the pope and the Council of Trent, the Church persecuted and burned at the stake millions who would not succumb to their edicts and dictates of the pope.

- At the Council of Trent in 1563 all previous beliefs were upheld and reinforced under penalty of death, including tradition superseding Scripture, salvation was not by "faith alone," the Mass was a real sacrifice of Jesus, purgatory was real, indulgences were freely available for a price, the jurisdiction of the pope was universal, and initiated the Counter-Reformation.

35 and some of the wise shall stumble, so that they may be refined, purified, and made white, until the time of the end, for it still awaits the appointed time.

- Recantation was used by some reformers to avoid death.

- *"until the time of the end, for it still awaits the appointed time"* is another specific reference to the time of the end in 1798.

Years of 1453—1798: Full Power and Authority of the Papacy (vv. 36–39)

36 And the king shall do as he wills. He shall exalt himself and magnify himself above every god, and shall speak astonishing things against the God of gods. He shall prosper till the indignation is accomplished; for what is decreed shall be done.

- The Papacy had reached the height of its power. The pope now headed the only Christian church-state system with the fall of Constantinople. The Church was able to make political rulers conform to their wishes by the threat of ex-communication, and used the Church's own temporal power as a state power to persecute the Protestants. And finally, the pope himself, acting with and through his councils, has issued edicts, he has attacked the holy covenant by controverting the plan of salvation, and by instituting the Eucharist; he has profaned and replaced the daily sanctuary service by instituting the Rosary and prayers to Mary and the saints, forbidding the reading and possession of the Bible, and instituting a system of salvation by works.

- Finally, the Catholic Church changed God's commandants by removing the second and allowing for image worship and replacing the fourth with Sunday worship. The earthly power of the Holy See, the Church of Rome, will continue until 1798, when the indignation against its outrages, overreach, and malign influence reaches its fill.

37 He shall pay no attention to the gods of his fathers, or to the one beloved by women. He shall not pay attention to any other god, for he shall magnify himself above all.

- Here we see the Papacy elevating tradition and councils over the Bible, the Word of God, and promoting celibacy. In the mid-sixteenth century, Pope Pius V stated, "The Pope and God are the same, so he has all power in Heaven and earth."

- This *"god his fathers did not know"* refers to traditions, council canons, veneration of Mary, and Papal Bulls that have come in and replaced the Word of God.

- In 1074, Pope Gregory VII championed priestly celibacy with his published encyclical forbidding the priests and clergy from marrying and commanding them to stay celibate.

38 He shall honor the god of fortresses instead of these. A god whom his fathers did not know he shall honor with gold and silver, with precious stones and costly gifts.

- This *"god of fortresses"* can be seen in the pope's temporal power not only with the Jesuits, Dominicans, and Papal Army but the powers of Catholic nations. Instead of using a "thus sayeth the Lord," the Papacy used a "thus sayeth the blade."

- Much of the money parishioners paid for indulgence went to pay for massive cathedrals adorned with gold and precious stones of images of Mary and the Saints to be worshiped.

39 He shall deal with the strongest fortresses with the help of a foreign god. Those who acknowledge him he shall load with honor. He shall make them rulers over many and shall divide the land for a price.

- *"foreign god"* could be Mary and her doing the CoRedemtrix with Jesus and the belief she was taken to heaven without sin.

- The distribution of land for a price can be seen in the church's property holdings throughout the world.

- In 1493, Pope Alexander VI issued the Papal Bull *Inter Caetera* or "Among other," divided trading and colonizing rights between Portugal and Spain (Castile), excluding other European nations such as England and Netherlands. The following year, Spain and Portugal signed the Treaty of Tordesillas. The New World was ripe for Catholic conversion, and the pope declared King Ferdinand of Spain an apostolic vicar in the Indies.

Years 1798—Second Coming of Jesus: Papal Power at the End of Time (Dan. 11:40–45)

40 At the time of the end, the king of the south shall attack him, but the king of the north shall rush upon him like a whirlwind, with chariots and horsemen, and with many ships. And he shall come into countries and shall overflow and pass through.

- In 1798, Revolutionary France took Pope Pius VI captive and exiled him. This ended the Papal rule during the Divided Kingdoms and the 1260 and 1290-year prophecies that started in 508 with the crowning of Clovis.

- The resurrected temporal power of Roman Catholicism has in these last days been pronounced and it is universally respected as the mouthpiece of both the Catholic and Protestant churches. This began in 1929 with the Lateran Treaty when Italy gave the Vatican temporal power with the Vatican nation. The Vatican received diplomatic relations from nations all over the world, including an ambassador from the United States in 1983. It will soon combine forces with the United States to reinforce its dogmas of the medieval period against the holy covenant.

- The pattern over time, starting with President Reagan, shows an ever-increasing relationship between the Vatican and the United States. This path is leading to a combining of forces to reinforce its dogmas, just as was seen in the medieval period.

41 He shall come into the glorious land. And tens of thousands shall fall, but these shall be delivered out of his hand: Edom and Moab and the main part of the Ammonites.

- In 2015, we witnessed Pope Francis standing in the well of the U.S. Congress and his address the world at the United Nations. While this may not be the exact fulfillment of the prophecy regarding the Vatican coming with power into Protestant lands, it is patently obvious where the trajectory is headed in regard to a union of church and state.

- Edom, Moab, and the Ammonites were ancient relatives of the Jews. In the final days, when the full intentions of the Vatican will be revealed, many from the various Protestant churches will come out and take their stand with God's end-time people.

42 He shall stretch out his hand against the countries, and the land of Egypt shall not escape.

- The Vatican and the United States will work hand-in-hand to force the entire world to bow to Vatican dogmas against God's covenant.

43 He shall become ruler of the treasures of gold and of silver, and all the precious things of Egypt, and the Libyans and the Cushites shall follow in his train.

- Vatican authority and power will sweep the world over, including groups of atheism, paganism, and Eastern religions.

44 But news from the east and the north shall alarm him, and he shall go out with great fury to destroy and devote many to destruction.

- The loud cry of the authentic Scriptural covenant message pressing all inhabitants to choose between standing with God and His people in keeping His Ten Commandment Law and holding to the Bible alone or standing with the counterfeit mark and the Catholic Church.

- At this time, God's people experience a situation similar to that found in Daniel 3, where they must refuse to accept the counterfeit image.

45 And he shall pitch his palatial tents between the sea and the glorious holy mountain. Yet he shall come to his end, with none to help him.

- This glorious mountain is Jesus's kingdom and His people. This same mountain was seen in Daniel 2:35, where we read, *"But the stone that struck the image became a great mountain and filled the whole earth."*

- Enraged, the Vatican will coerce the United States and the world to pass a death decree against Michael's people—those who keep God's commandments.

- At this point, God's people experience a situation similar to that found in Daniel 6, where they must continue to worship despite a death decree.

- Like in the time of Esther, just before the date the decree is to be carried out, the Vatican power will come to its end.

Daniel 12:1 is the conclusion of the prophecy of Chapter 11

1 At that time shall arise Michael, the great prince who has charge of your people. And there shall be a time of trouble, such as never has been since there was a nation till that time. But at that time your people shall be delivered, everyone whose name shall be found written in the book.

- Probation closed on the Jewish nation in AD 34 when Stephan was stoned, and Jesus stood up, pronounced the Jewish nation "guilty," and closed the court case in God vs. the Jewish nation. When this final death on God's people falls, probation closes. Michael/Jesus will stand up, pronounce the Vatican church-state system "guilty," and close the court case in God vs. the church-state system of the Vatican, giving judgment in favor of God's covenant-keeping people.

Appendix B: Time Prophecy Chart

THERE ARE SEVERAL time prophecies in Daniel chapters 7, 8, 9, and 12. Daniel 11 does not have a time prophecy, yet it does have several verses corresponding to these prophetic dates. Using the day-year principle, each day in a prophecy equals one literal year.

For more information on the day for a year principle, see the article by Clifford Goldstein, "The day-year principle: The amazing day-year key can still unlock the prophecies of Daniel and Revelation," in *Ministry* magazine, 2018, https://www.ministrymagazine.org/archive/2018/04/The-day-year-principle.

Below in the chart, we see the prophecy, the corresponding event description in Daniel, and the historical event.

Time Prophecy	Corresponding Event Prophecy	Historical Event
"Time, times, and ½ a times" Daniel 7 and 12	Daniel 7:24 *"As for the ten horns, out of this kingdom ten kings shall arise, and another shall arise after them"* Daniel 7:26 *"But the court shall sit in judgment, and his dominion shall be taken away, to be consumed and destroyed to the end."*	This began in 538 when the Papacy had all three elements to rule Christendom: a temporal power arm: (AD 508 Frankish kingdom), authority (AD 533 the letter from the Emperor), and domination to operate from the defeat of the Ostrogoths from Rome (AD 538). It ended in 1798 when the French Directory ordered General Berthier to capture and exile the pope, removing his temporal authority.
2300 Days Daniel 8	Daniel 8:14, *"And he said to me, 'For 2,300 evenings and mornings. Then the sanctuary shall be restored to its rightful state.'"*	This is the heavenly Day of Atonement, which began 2,300 years from the Decree of Artaxerxes in 457 BC. In 1844, Jesus, our High Priest, entered the Most Holy Place in heaven.

70 Weeks Daniel 9	Daniel 8:24, *"Seventy weeks are* *decreed about your* *people and your holy* *city, to finish the* *transgression, to put* *an end to sin, and* *to atone for iniquity,* *to bring in ever-* *lasting righteousness,* *to seal both vision* *and prophet, and* *to anoint a most* *holy place.*	Our starting point is the same as the 2,300 Days with the decree Artaxerxes decree in 457 BC. Jesus started His earthly ministry in week 70, which was AD 27 at His baptism. In the middle of the week or in AD 31, He was crucified and ended the sacrificial service. Then in AD 34, at the end of the week, after Stephan's defense before the Jewish Sanhedrin, he was stoned and the 70-week probationary period for the Jews closed.
1290 Days Daniel 12	Daniel 11:23, *"And* *from the time that* *an alliance is made* *with him he shall act* *deceitfully, and he* *shall become strong* *with a small people."*	This time period links with Daniel 7 and the *time, times, and half of* *time,* which ended in 1798, so if we move back 1290 years, we come to AD 508 and find an alli- ance with the king of the Franks and the Papacy that would last until 1798.

| 1335 Days
Daniel 12 | Daniel 11:23, *"And from the time that an alliance is made with him he shall act deceitfully, and he shall become strong with a small people."* | This time period links with Daniel 8 and the *2,300-days,* which ended in 1844. Daniel 12:12, *"Blessed is he who waits and arrives at the 1,335 days."* In AD 508, Catholicism was given a militant arm to carry out its anti-sanctuary ministry dogmas against God's true people. Even so, the year 1843 brought a blessing to God's people, free from Papal persecution and a steadfast belief that Jesus was returning in the following year to "cleanse the sanctuary." |

CPSIA information can be obtained
at www.ICGtesting.com
Printed in the USA
JSHW012357200722
28361JS00004B/17